BRANCH

	DATE DUE		

Other Titles of Interest by Jim Wiese

Roller Coaster Science

50 Wet, Wacky, Wild, Dizzy Experiments
about Things Kids Like Best

Rocket Science

50 Flying, Floating, Flipping, Spinning Gadgets
Kids Create Themselves

Detective Science

40 Crime-Solving, Case-Breaking, Crook-Catching
Activities for Kids

Spy Science

40 Secret-Sleuthing, Code-Cracking, Spy-Catching
Activities for Kids

Cosmic Science

Over 40 Gravity-Defying, Earth-Orbiting, Space-Cruising Activities for Kids

Jim Wiese

Illustrations by Tina Cash-Walsh

John Wiley & Sons, Inc.

New York • Chichester • Weinheim • Brisbane • Singapore • Toronto

Copyright © 1997 by Jim Wiese
Published by John Wiley & Sons, Inc.

Illustrations © 1997 by Tina Cash-Walsh

Library of Congress Catatloging-in-Publication Data

Wiese, Jim
    Cosmic science: over 40 gravity-defying, earth-orbiting, space-cruising activities for kids / Jim Wiese.
       p.   cm.
    Includes index.
    Summary: Provides instructions for activities exploring gravity, moon craters, the planets of our solar system, and other aspects of outer space.
       ISBN 0-471-15852-6 (pbk. : alk. paper)
    1. Outer space—Exploration—Experiments—Juvenile literature. 2. Astronomy—Experiments—Juvenile literature. [1. Outer space—Experiments. 2. Astronomy—Experiments. 3. Experiments.] I. Title.
    QB500.22.W54   1997
    629.4'078—dc20   96-34528
                                                                                    CIP
                                                                                     AC

Printed in the United States of America
10 9 8 7 6 5 4 3 2 1

For Matthew,

who always looks to the stars

Acknowledgments

The idea for this book probably began when my son was in elementary school and couldn't decide whether he was going to be an NBA basketball player or an astronaut when he grew up. Maybe, he thought, he'd become both. The game of basketball would certainly be different with a franchise on the Moon! From those first talks, Matthew and I have shared a common interest in space and astronomy over the years. From *Star Trek* and *The Next Generation* to the flight of *Voyager* and, more recently, *Galileo*'s encounter with Jupiter, we have both been interested in what's out there. The idea of doing a book about space and space travel came initially from Matthew's interest in the topic. When my daughter, Elizabeth, also showed similar interest in space, I thought the topic deserved a book on its own.

Special thanks on this book go to the whole Wiley team, who make sure that my ideas are expressed in the best possible way. Kate Bradford and Kara Raezer continue to support my efforts as a writer, and I'm very appreciative.

The person who deserves the most credit for this book is my wife, Barbara, who continues to support my writing.

Contents

Introduction

Have you ever looked up at the stars and wondered whether anyone or anything up there were looking back at you? Have you thought about being an astronaut and traveling to worlds beyond our own, exploring where no one has gone before? Do you know how rockets launch, or how astronauts work without gravity or move around on the Moon? If you've wondered about these and other questions about space, then this book is for you. Exploring space is exciting and fun. So get ready for these tantalizing experiments and activities to take you out of this world!

How to Use This Book

This book is full of information and simple science experiments that will help you discover more about space. The book is divided into the following subjects: Understanding Our Solar System, Rocketing out of Earth's Gravity, Orbiting Earth, Living and Working in Space, Walking on the Moon, Probing the Planets, and Seeing the Stars and More. In each chapter, there are groups of projects that teach you about a specific idea. Each project has a list of materials and a procedure to follow. You'll be able to find most of the materials needed around the house or at your neighborhood hardware or grocery store. Some of the projects have a section called More Fun Stuff to Do, which lets you try different variations on the original activity. An explanation is given at the end of each project. Words in **bold** type are defined in the Glossary at the back of the book.

Being a Good Scientist

- Read through the instructions once completely and collect all the equipment you'll need before you start the activity or experiment.

- Keep a notebook. Write down what you do for your experiment or project and what happens.

- Follow the instructions carefully. *Do not attempt to do any steps yourself that require the help of an adult.*

- If your experiment or project doesn't work properly the first time, try again or try doing it in a slightly different way. In real life, experiments don't always work out perfectly the first time.

- Always have an open mind that asks questions and looks for answers. The basis of good science is asking good questions and finding the best answers.

Increasing Your Understanding

- Make small changes in the design of the equipment or project to see whether the results stay the same. Change only one thing at a time so you can tell which change caused a particular result.

- Make up an experiment or activity to test your own ideas about how things work.

- Look at the things around you for examples of the scientific principles that you've learned.

- Don't worry if at first you don't understand the things around you. There are always new things to discover. Remember that many of the most famous discoveries were made by accident.

Using This Book to Do a Science Fair Project

Many of the activities in this book can serve as the starting point for a science fair project. After doing the experiment as it is written in the book, what questions come to mind? Some possible projects are suggested in the section of the activities called More Fun Stuff to Do.

To begin your science fair project, first write down the problem you want to study and come up with a hypothesis. A **hypothesis** is an educated guess about the results of an experiment you are going to perform. The purpose of a hypothesis is to give a possible explanation of how something happens. For example, if you enjoyed the Plants in Orbit investigation (Chapter 3, Project 6), you may want to find out how other plants grow in similar situations. A hypothesis for this experiment could be that smaller plants grow better in orbit than larger plants.

To test your hypothesis, first create an experiment. In the Plants in Orbit investigation, you'll want to try growing plants of different sizes, like bush beans and corn, to see how spinning affects their growth. Be sure to keep careful records of your experiment. Next, analyze the data you recorded. In the Plants in Orbit investigation, you could create a table showing the days since planting, including changes in the height, shape, and growth direction of your plants, or you could make a graph to show the results. Finally, come up with a conclusion that shows how your results prove or disprove your hypothesis.

This process is called the **scientific method**. When following the scientific method, you begin with a hypothesis, test it with an experiment, analyze the results, and draw a conclusion.

A Word of Warning

Some science experiments can be dangerous. *Ask an adult to help you with experiments that call for adult help, such as those that involve matches, knives, or other dangerous materials.* Don't forget to ask an adult's permission to use household items, and put away your equipment and clean up your work area when you have finished experimenting. Good scientists are careful and avoid accidents.

1

Before You Go

Understanding Our Solar System

All trips start at the beginning. Before you take a trip into outer space, you need to begin by understanding astronomy. **Astronomy** is the branch of science that studies the **stars** (spinning balls of hot gas that release energy in the form of heat and light), **planets** (objects that travel around stars), and other objects in space. An **astronomer** is an expert in astronomy.

When the first astronomers looked into space, they used only their eyes. They tracked the path of the Moon and studied the location of the stars. But they wanted to learn more. In 1609, the Italian astronomer Galileo Galilei (1564–1642) first used a telescope to study space. (A **telescope** is a tubelike instrument that uses lenses to make distant objects appear nearer and larger.)

Astronomers like Galileo eventually learned many things about Earth in space. They learned that Earth is located in a solar system. (A **solar system** is a star with a group of planets and other objects traveling around it.) The star in the center of a solar system is a sun. Our sun is called the **Sun**. Revolving around our sun are nine planets: Mercury, Venus, Earth, Mars, Jupiter, Saturn, Uranus, Neptune, and Pluto. Some planets, like Earth, have one or more **moons**, which are objects that travel around a planet. Earth's moon is called the Moon.

But just learning about the stars, planets, and moons from Earth was eventually not enough for astronomers. They wanted to visit the places they had previously viewed only through a telescope.

This book will take you on an imaginary trip into space. But before you go, try the following activities to learn more about astronomy.

Project 1
MIRROR, MIRROR

Many years ago, people thought Earth was flat. They thought the Sun and Moon moved around Earth while Earth stood still. Then the first astronomers discovered that Earth is a round ball that moves. Try the following activity to "see" how Earth moves.

Materials

small mirror
masking tape
timer

Procedure

NOTE: This activity works best on sunny days.

1. Lay the mirror faceup on the sill of a window that faces south. Position the mirror so that the Sun **reflects** (bounces back) onto one of the walls of the room.

2. At exactly 12:00 noon, place a small loop of masking tape on the wall in the center of the mirror's reflection.

3. Every 5 minutes, for 30 minutes, place another small loop of tape in the center of the reflection. What do you notice after 30 minutes?

4. Leave the mirror undisturbed overnight. At exactly 12:00 noon the next day, place a small loop of tape on the wall in the center of the reflection.

5. For the next 2 weeks, place a small loop of tape on the wall in the center of the reflection each day at exactly 12:00 noon. What do you notice after 2 weeks?

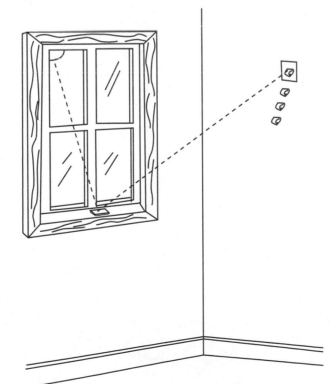

Explanation

In the first 24 hours, the reflection moves across the wall in a straight line. The reflection moves because Earth spins. Earth makes one complete turn on its **axis** (an imaginary line that runs through the North and South poles of Earth) every 24 hours. (The **North Pole** is the northernmost point of Earth, and the **South Pole** is the southern-most point.) As Earth turns, the angle that the Sun makes with the mirror changes, causing the reflection to move.

When you place a piece of tape in the center of the reflection at the same time each day for 2 weeks, you notice that the reflection moves each day as well. (The new reflection is either higher or lower than the previous reflection, depending on the season. The new reflection will be higher in the fall and lower in the spring.) The reflection moves each day because Earth doesn't just spin on its axis. It also **orbits** the Sun, which means it moves in a circular path around the Sun. Earth makes one complete circle around the Sun each year, spinning as it orbits.

Earth is slightly tilted as it orbits the Sun in a counterclockwise direction. As Earth spins, its axis is tilted 23½ degrees (23½°). This means that for half of its trip around the Sun, the **Northern Hemisphere** (top half of Earth) is tilted toward the Sun, and for the other half, it is tilted away from the Sun.

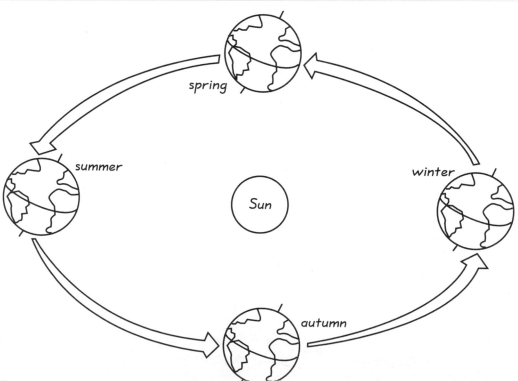

This tilting creates our seasons. If you live in the Northern Hemisphere, it's winter when the top half of Earth is tilted away from the Sun. It's summer when the top half of Earth is tilted toward the Sun. When the top half of Earth is tilted neither away from nor toward the Sun, it's either spring or fall.

Project 2
MAN IN THE MOON

When we look at the Moon from Earth, sometimes it looks round and full, and other times we see only a curved edge of the Moon called a **crescent**. Why does the shape of the Moon appear to change? Try the next activity to find out.

Materials

lamp with shade removed

yardstick (meterstick)

baskctball

Proccdure

NOTE: This activity works best at night.

1. Place the lamp on a table in the center of the room. Turn on the lamp and turn off all other lights in the room.

2. Stand about 10 feet (3 m) from the lightbulb, facing away from the bulb.

3. Hold the ball at arm's length in front of you so that the light strikes the ball. Move the ball slightly left or right if your body blocks the light from the bulb. How much of the ball is lighted?

4. Holding the ball at arm's length, slowly begin to turn to your left (counterclockwise). Stop after making a quarter turn. You should be standing sideways in relation to the lamp. How much of the ball is lighted now?

5. Make another quarter turn so that you are facing the lamp. Now how much of the ball is lighted?

Cosmic Science in Action

On May 25, 1961, President John F. Kennedy (1917–1963) set a goal for the U.S. space program: to land a man on the Moon and return him safely to Earth. The **National Aeronautics and Space Administration (NASA),** the organization that oversees the U.S. space program, successfully reached that goal with the Apollo program and Neil Armstrong's first steps on the Moon in 1969. The Apollo program used a three-man Apollo spacecraft attached to a Saturn rocket. NASA launched 15 manned Apollo flights. Eleven of these were missions in the **lunar** (relating to the Moon) program, including six Moon landings.

Explanation

In this activity, the lamp represents the Sun, the ball represents the Moon, and you represent Earth. When the Moon is on the opposite side of Earth from the Sun (when you are facing away from the lamp), the Moon is completely lit and appears full. This is called a full moon.

When the Moon is beside Earth (when you are standing sideways), only half of its lighted surface can be seen from Earth. This is called a quarter moon. When the Moon is between Earth and the Sun (when you are facing the lamp), the lighted surface cannot be seen from Earth. This is called a new moon.

Our Moon is a spinning ball of rock with no air or water. It's also a natural **satellite** (an object that orbits a planet) of Earth. Our Moon orbits Earth about once every 28 days. However, it also makes one complete turn on its axis during that same time. This means that the same side of the Moon always faces Earth, and we never see its dark side.

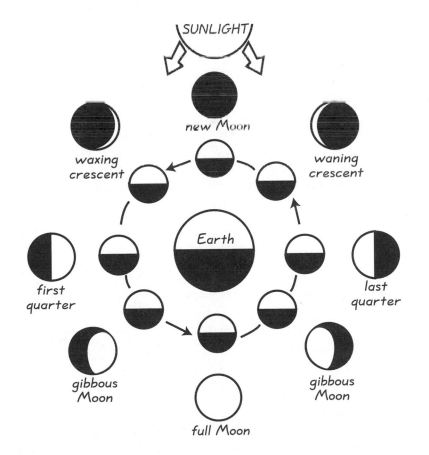

Project 3
SUN POWER

We don't usually think of the Sun as a star, but it is. All stars, including the Sun, are spinning balls of hot gas that release energy as heat and light. Although it's very important to us, the Sun is only an average-size star. Still, it's very powerful. How much power does the Sun have? Try the next investigation to find out.

Materials

lamp with a 100-watt bulb

extension cord long enough to reach outdoors

metric ruler

calculator or pencil and paper

Procedure

NOTE: This activity must be performed outdoors on a warm, sunny day.

CAUTION: Do not touch the lightbulb.

1. Find an area where direct sunlight is next to shade, such as the corner of a house or next to a tree.

2. Place the lamp in the shade. Use the extension cord to plug the lamp into an indoor electric outlet, and turn the lamp on.

3. Place your hand in direct sunlight so that your palm faces the Sun. Feel the heat that the Sun produces.

4. Place your palm near the lamp's bulb until you find a position where the heat of the bulb feels equal to the heat of the Sun. Check this by moving your hand from the sunlight to the lamp several times, until you are sure that you feel the same heat from the bulb as from the Sun.

5. Use the ruler to measure the distance from your hand to the bulb in centimeters.

6. Calculate the Sun's power with a calculator or a pencil and paper by the following steps:

- Multiply the distance from your hand to the bulb by itself. For example, if your hand is 8 cm from the lightbulb, multiply 8 cm by 8 cm to get 64.

- Divide 225 by that number.
  $225 \div 64 = 3.5$

- Multiply that number by 10^{26} to get the power of the Sun in watts. (A **watt** is the unit used to measure power.) (10^{26} means a 1 with 26 zeros after it, or 100,000,000,000,000,000,000,000,000.)

  3.5×10^{26} watts = 350,000,000,000,000,000,000,000,000 watts

Explanation

The Sun is a huge, spinning ball of very hot gas, mostly hydrogen. At the center of the sun, a reaction called **nuclear fusion** occurs, which changes hydrogen gas into helium gas and releases a great deal of energy. That energy is sent out in all directions as light and heat.

The palm of your hand is a reasonably good detector of heat energy. By using your hand to compare the Sun's heat to the heat of a 100-watt lightbulb, you can calculate the power of the Sun fairly accurately. You should have calculated the Sun's total power output, called **luminosity** (the total power output from any sun or star), to be approximately 3.9×10^{26} watts.

The Sun uses up 300 million tons (600 billion kg) of hydrogen gas each second to create 390,000,000,000,000,000,000,000,000 watts of power. That may sound like a lot, but the Sun has enough hydrogen left to last at least 5 billion years.

Project 4
BODE'S LAW

Our solar system is made up of the Sun, and the planets that travel around it. Each planet in our solar system is a different distance from the Sun. Can you think of a way to figure out how far away each is? (You can't exactly measure the distance with a ruler!) Try the following activity to see how a young German astronomer named Johann Bode (1747–1826) did it.

Materials

pencil

paper

Procedure

1. Copy the chart below onto the paper.

Planet	I Starting numbers (each number after 0 is twice the number before)	II Add 4	III Sum divided by 10 (Bode's predicted distance)	IV Actual measured distance from Sun in AU	V Average distance from Sun measured in millions of km (miles)
Mercury	0	4	0.4	0.39	58 (36)
Venus	3			0.72	108 (67)
Earth	6			1.0	150 (93)
Mars	12			1.5	228 (142)
Missing Planet	24			2.8	—
Jupiter				5.2	778 (484)
Saturn				9.5	1,427 (887)
Uranus				19.2	2,870 (1,800)
Neptune				30.1	4,486 (2,781)
Pluto				39.5	5,900 (3,658)

2. Complete the following steps to fill out the chart:

- Fill out column I by giving each planet a starting number in the order listed. Give Mercury a 0, Venus a 3, and each planet a number that is double the number before it.

- Fill out column II by adding 4 to each starting number.

- Fill out column III by dividing each number in column II by 10. This gives Bode's distance in **astronomical units (AUs)**. One AU is equal to the distance from the Sun to Earth.

3. Compare Bode's distances in column III to the actual distances of the planets to the Sun measured in AUs in column IV. How accurate is Bode's law for all the planets?

Explanation

In the late 1700s, Johann Bode popularized a simple mathematical equation for finding the distance of each planet from the Sun, which is now called **Bode's law**. Bode's law gave the distance from the Sun of the known planets in our solar system and predicted where future planets would be located. At the time Bode's law was first discovered, the planets were known only as far as Saturn. Bode used Bode's law to predict the next planet in the solar system and its location. In 1781 a planet was discovered by British astronomer William Herschel (1738–1822) in the location that Bode predicted. The planet was named Uranus as suggested by Bode.

Bode's law was also useful because it predicted that a planet lay between Mars and Jupiter. In 1801 astronomers turned their telescopes where Bode predicted the missing planet would be and found instead an asteroid that they named Ceres. (An **asteroid** is a small, rocky planet that orbits the Sun.) Later, they discovered that there were

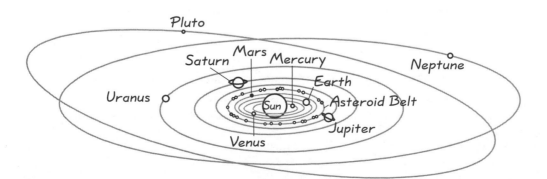

thousands of asteroids, ranging in size from 600 to 0.6 miles (1,000 to 1 km) in diameter, in that location. These asteroids travel in an orbit between Mars and Jupiter called the **asteroid belt.**

Although Bode's law did help astronomers find new planets (and the asteroid belt) in our solar system, most scientists feel that Bode's law is not a law of nature but rather a coincidence. As you discovered in this activity, the law is more accurate closer to the Sun, where more planets are located.

Project 5
TOILET PAPER PLANETS

Use Bode's distances and a roll of toilet paper to map the solar system.

Materials

pencil

paper

your chart from the previous activity, Bode's law

marking pen

ten 3-by-5-inch (7.5-by-12.5-cm) index cards

roll of toilet paper

Procedure

NOTE: Procedure should be performed outdoors in a large, flat area.

1. List all of the planets in order on the sheet of paper. For the missing planet, write ASTEROIDS.

2. For each planet, multiply each of the distances in column IV of your chart by 10. Round each product to the nearest whole number and write the result next to the appropriate planet. (Check your results on the next page.)

3. Using the marking pen, write the name of a each planet, except Pluto, on each card. Make a card for the asteroids and one for the Sun.

4. Go outside and begin to unroll the toilet paper. Place the card for the Sun at the starting end of the paper.

5. Place the next card, Mercury, on the fourth square of toilet paper.

6. Place the next card, Venus, on the seventh square of toilet paper.

7. Continue to unroll the toilet paper, placing each planet's card on the square of toilet paper that corresponds to that planet's number on the chart.

8. Stop when you reach Neptune. (There are usually only 300 sheets on a roll of toilet paper, not enough to include Pluto.) Are the planets evenly spaced in the solar system? Where are most of them located?

Explanation

Your chart for the distances should look like the one shown.

When you map the planets in the solar system, you notice that they are not equally spaced. The first four planets—Mercury, Venus, Earth, and Mars—are relatively close to one another and to the Sun. After Mars, the planets become farther and farther apart. There are enormous distances between Jupiter, Saturn, Uranus, Neptune, and Pluto. Light from the Sun takes 3 minutes to reach Mercury and 8 minutes to reach Earth, but it takes 5½ hours to reach Pluto.

Mercury	4
Venus	7
Earth	10
Mars	15
Asteroids	28
Jupiter	52
Saturn	95
Uranus	192
Neptune	301
Pluto	395

Like Earth, the planets all spin as they orbit the Sun. All the planets except Mercury and Venus have moons that orbit them. Jupiter has 16 moons.

COSMIC SCIENCE IN ACTION

On July 4, 1997, a collection of computers, lasers, and cameras is scheduled to land on the surface of Mars. This will be the first of five missions planned over the next decade as part of the Mars Global Surveyor Program. The Mars landing vehicle, nicknamed *Rocky,* weighs 23 pounds (10.4 kg) and takes up as much space as a microwave oven. It will roll around the surface of Mars at a rate of 1/2 inch (1.25 cm) per second, taking pictures and analyzing rocks and soil. Scientists hope this information will reveal the history of Mars's climate.

Project 6
CIRCLING THE SUN

Most people think that Earth and the other planets in our solar system orbit the Sun by moving in perfect circles. But that's not the case. Try the following activity to learn about their orbits.

Materials

transparent tape
8½-by-11-inch (21.25-by-27.5-cm) sheet of typing paper
cardboard or corkboard
pencil
ruler
2 pushpins
12-inch (30-cm) piece of string

Procedure

1. Tape the paper to the cardboard.

2. In the middle of the paper, draw a horizontal line about 3 inches (7.5 cm) long. Stick a pushpin into the paper at each end of the line.

3. Tie the ends of the string together to make a loop.

4. Loop the string over the pushpins.

5. Place the pencil point against the inside of the loop.

6. Keeping the string taut, you guide the pencil around the inside of the loop to draw a shape. What shape does it make?

Explanation

You have drawn an oval-shaped figure called an **ellipse**. The planets in our solar system move around the Sun in elliptical orbits.

In 1621, German astronomer Johannes Kepler (1571–1630) discovered that the planets don't orbit the Sun in perfect circles and don't move at a constant speed. Kepler discovered that the planets orbit the Sun in ellipses and move at different speeds. They move faster when near the Sun and slower farther from it.

Kepler worked out precise laws to explain exactly how the planets orbit the Sun. But it was not for another 66 years that anyone could explain why the planets move at different speeds. In 1687, the English scientist Isaac Newton (1642–1727) published his famous theory of gravitation. He explained that planets were held in their orbits by a **force** (a push or pull on an object). That force is **gravity,** which is the force of attraction between two objects due to their **mass** (the amount of matter in an object).

The force of gravity between the Sun and the planets is what keeps them orbiting the Sun. However, gravity's effect decreases with distance, which is why planets move slower the farther they are from the Sun.

Blast Off!

Rocketing out of Earth's Gravity

To actually travel in space, you have to first escape Earth's gravity. Gravity is what attracts all objects to Earth and gives them weight. (**Weight** is actually the force with which objects are pulled toward Earth.) You are held to Earth by gravity unless you can create enough force to overcome the force of gravity.

To escape Earth's gravity, you must travel at a speed of 25,000 miles per hour (40,000 kph). This speed is called **escape velocity**, the speed needed to escape a planet's gravity. The only engines strong enough to create this kind of speed are **rockets.** Rockets use tremendous amounts of fuel to work, so most of a rocket is made of fuel. The rest of the rocket is payload, the satellites, or the **space capsule** (the top part of a rocket that holds the astronauts).

Until recently, all rockets could be used only once since all parts of the rocket except the space capsule were destroyed after takeoff. Today, however, American astronauts travel in the reusable space shuttle. The shuttle has a giant fuel tank that is separate from the part of the shuttle that carries the astronauts and satellites. The fuel tank cannot be reused, but the rest of the shuttle can.

To learn more about rockets and how to break the hold of Earth's gravity, try the next activities.

Project 1
PULL OF THE EARTH

To understand how to escape Earth's gravity, you first need to understand how gravity works. Try the following activity to investigate the force of Earth's gravity on different objects.

Materials

magazine

2 sheets of 8½-by-11-inch (21.25-by-27.5-cm) paper

Procedure

1. Hold the magazine and a sheet of paper at arm's length in front of you. They should be about the same distance from the floor.

2. Drop both objects at the same time. Which object reaches the ground first?

3. Crumple the second sheet of paper into a small ball.

4. Repeat steps 1 and 2, replacing the flat sheet of paper with the crumpled paper. Now which object reaches the ground first? Does the weight of the object affect the time it takes to fall to the ground?

Explanation

When you drop the magazine and a flat sheet of paper at the same time, the magazine reaches the ground first. As you release the objects, gravity pulls them toward the ground. However, tiny, invisible, moving particles of air called **air molecules**, bump against the falling objects. The opposing force of these air molecules against falling

objects is called **air resistance**. Air resistance has a greater effect on the sheet of paper than on the magazine because the sheet of paper weighs less than the magazine.

However, when you crumple the sheet of paper into a ball and drop it at the same time as the magazine, they both reach the ground at the same time. This is because you have reduced the effect of air resistance on the paper by crumpling it. The ball of paper meets with less air resistance than the flat sheet of paper.

Gravity is the main force acting on the magazine and the paper. When you take away the effect of air resistance, both the piece of paper and the magazine fall at the same speed and reach the ground at the same time. Without the effect of air resistance, gravity causes all objects to fall at the same speed when dropped from the same height, no matter what they weigh.

When you place the sheet of paper on top of the magazine, the magazine blocks the air resistance on the sheet of paper and the paper falls at the same speed as the magazine. Similarly, when you place the sheet of paper below the magazine, the magazine eliminates the air resistance on the sheet of paper and the paper again falls at the same speed as the magazine. If weight of the magazine were the only force pushing the flat sheet of paper down, then when the paper was on top of the magazine, the magazine would fall faster than the sheet of paper.

Gravity is the main force acting on the magazine and the paper. When you take away the effect of air resistance, both the piece of paper and the magazine fall at the same speed and reach the ground at the same time. Without the effect of air resistance, gravity causes all objects to fall at the same speed when dropped from the same height, no matter what they weigh.

Project 2
ALL FALL DOWN

Objects are pulled to Earth by the force of gravity. As you saw in the last activity, two objects dropped from the same height fall to Earth at the same speed. But do the objects fall at a constant speed, or does the speed increase as they fall? Investigate this question in the following activity.

Materials

10 beads
two 8-foot (2.4-m) pieces of string
yardstick (meterstick)
marking pen
metal cookie sheet
chair

Procedure

1. Attach one bead to the end of one string by threading the string through the bead and tying a knot on either side of the bead to hold it in place.

2. Measure 2 feet (0.6 m) from the first bead, and make a mark. Attach a second bead, then add three more beads, spacing them 2 feet (0.6 m) apart.

3. Attach one bead to the end of the other string. Attach four more beads to the string at distances of 6 inches (15 cm), 24 inches (60 cm), 54 inches (137 cm), and 96 inches (244 cm) from the first bead.

4. Place the cookie sheet on the floor next to the chair.

5. Stand on the chair, holding the first string of beads so that the bottom bead is over the cookie sheet.

6. Drop the first string of beads and listen to the sound of the beads as they hit the sheet.

7. Repeat steps 5 and 6 with the second string of beads. How is the sound of the second string of beads different from the sound of the first string?

Explanation

Although the beads are evenly spaced along the first string, when you drop the first string of beads, the time intervals between sounds get shorter as the string falls. When you drop the second string however, the time intervals between sounds stay the same the whole time.

This is because falling objects **accelerate** (speed up) as they fall. Due to the force of gravity, the longer an object falls, the faster it goes. The top beads on the string must fall longer than the lower beads. Thus, the top beads travel faster and cover larger distances in a shorter time than the lower beads.

On the first string, all the beads travel the same distance of 2 feet (0.6 m), but the top beads travel that distance faster than the lower beads. This is why the time intervals between sounds get shorter as the string falls. The beads of the second string are strung farther and farther apart, so the top beads must travel farther than the lower beads. The longer distances the top beads must travel make up for their increasing speed. Thus all of the beads on the second string hit the cookie sheet at the same time interval. In other words, the distance between beads on the second string is equal to the **acceleration** (increase in speed) of the beads due to gravity.

Project 3
DON'T MISS!

Before a rocket can overcome the pull of gravity, it must first begin to move. For an object to move, it must overcome inertia. What is inertia? Try the following activity to find out.

Materials

plastic drinking glass
metal pie pan
toilet paper tube
golf ball
yardstick (meterstick)
broom

Procedure

CAUTION: You must use a *plastic* drinking glass. *Do not* substitute one made of glass.

1. Place the plastic glass near the edge of a table.

2. Center the pie pan right side up on top of the glass so that the pan sticks out over the edge of the table.

3. Center the toilet paper tube upright on the pie pan so that it is directly above the glass.

4. Place the golf ball on top of the toilet paper tube.

5. Hold the broom upright in front of you. Stand about 2 feet (0.6 m) from the golf ball tower, facing the tower.

6. Bend the broom's bristles toward you, then step on them to hold them to the floor.

7. Pull the broom toward you, then release it so that the broomstick hits the pie pan. What happens?

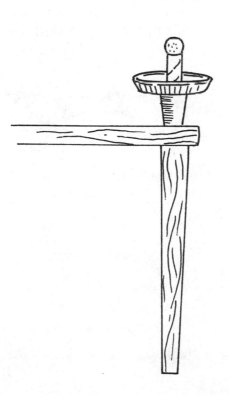
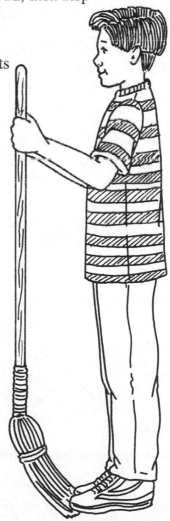

Once you have mastered this activity, try using an egg at the top of your tower instead of the golf ball. Fill the plastic drinking glass with water to keep the egg from breaking.

Explanation

This activity demonstrates **inertia,** which is the tendency of objects to resist a change in motion. The **law of inertia** states that an object at rest stays at rest and an object in motion stays in motion unless acted on by an outside force.

At first the golf ball is at rest, supported against the force of gravity by the pie pan and toilet paper tube. When you release the broom, it strikes the pie pan, creating an outside force on the pan. This force causes the pie pan to move away from the broom. Some of this force is transferred to the toilet paper tube, and it moves as well.

The glass and the golf ball are not acted on by the outside force, however, and they remain at rest. As soon as the pie pan and toilet paper tube are out of the way, gravity pulls the ball downward into the glass.

Project 4
PENNY PILE

Try another way to demonstrate the law of inertia.

Materials

25 pennies
metal spatula or wide, flat table knife

Procedure

1. Stack the pennies on a table.

2. Quickly slide the spatula along the table surface and knock the bottom penny out of the stack.

3. Knock each bottom penny out of the stack, using a very quick, but steady, back-and-forth motion.

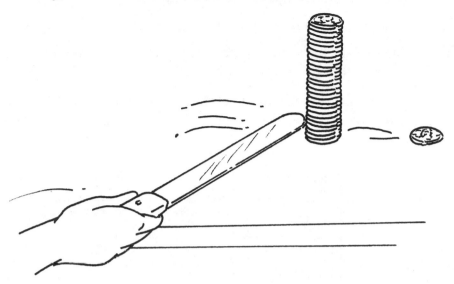

Explanation

When you strike the bottom penny, that penny is knocked from the stack, but the rest of the pennies stay stacked. The law of inertia states that objects at rest (like the stack of pennies) stay at rest unless acted on by an outside force. The only penny acted on by an outside force is the bottom one that you hit with the spatula. The other pennies remain at rest.

Project 5
ROCKET LAUNCHER

Now that you've learned about gravity and inertia, you need a rocket. All rockets work for the same reason. Try the next activity to learn how rockets work.

Materials

oblong balloon
20 feet (6 m) of string or nylon fishing line
drinking straw
2 chairs
transparent tape
scissors

Procedure

1. Blow up the balloon and tie the end in a knot.

2. Thread the string through the straw.

3. Tie the ends of the string to the chairs. The straw should move freely along the string.

4. Tape the balloon to the straw as shown. Position the balloon so that the knotted end is next to one of the chairs. Let go. What happens to the balloon?

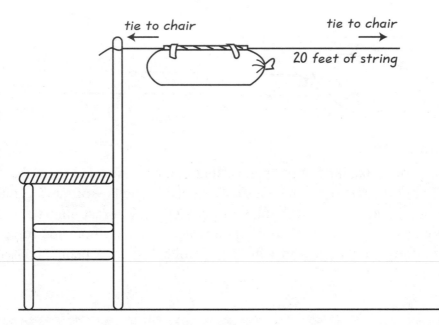

5. Leaving the balloon in place next to the chair, cut off the knotted end of the balloon with the scissors. What happens?

Explanation

All rockets, including the balloon rocket in this activity, work because of three laws of motion. These laws were put forward in 1687 by the English scientist Isaac Newton. You already know Newton's first law, which is the law of inertia. **Newton's three laws of motion** state:

1. An object at rest will stay at rest and an object in motion will stay in motion unless acted on by an outside force.

2. An object will move with an acceleration equal to the force applied to it.

3. For every action, there is an equal and opposite reaction.

In this experiment, at first the air inside the balloon pushes equally against the inside of the balloon. When the open end is cut or let go, the balloon pushes on the air inside, forcing it out the opening. This is the action force. In turn, the air pushes on the balloon. This is the reaction force. The reaction force, according to Newton's third law, is equal and in the opposite direction. It's the reaction force that pushes the balloon along the string. The more you blow up a balloon, the more force you create and the faster the balloon goes.

Like the balloon, rockets are launched due to action-reaction forces. Rocket engines produce gases that are pushed out the back of the rocket (the action). The gas applies a force on the rocket (the reaction), causing it to blast off.

The balloon rocket eventually stops moving. If an object stops, then according to Newton's first law, it must have a force acting against its movement. **Friction** is a force that slows down or stops the surfaces of objects from sliding over each other. Friction between the straw and

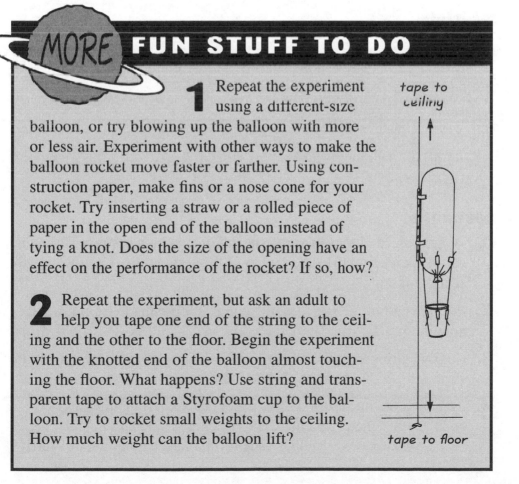

MORE FUN STUFF TO DO

1 Repeat the experiment using a different-size balloon, or try blowing up the balloon with more or less air. Experiment with other ways to make the balloon rocket move faster or farther. Using construction paper, make fins or a nose cone for your rocket. Try inserting a straw or a rolled piece of paper in the open end of the balloon instead of tying a knot. Does the size of the opening have an effect on the performance of the rocket? If so, how?

2 Repeat the experiment, but ask an adult to help you tape one end of the string to the ceiling and the other to the floor. Begin the experiment with the knotted end of the balloon almost touching the floor. What happens? Use string and transparent tape to attach a Styrofoam cup to the balloon. Try to rocket small weights to the ceiling. How much weight can the balloon lift?

tape to ceiling

tape to floor

the string and air resistance against the balloon (and weights in the Styrofoam cup in the More Fun Stuff to Do activity) are forces that act against the movement of the balloon. Without these opposing forces, the balloon rocket would keep moving.

In space there is little air resistance to stop spacecraft. A rocket engine gives the payload—often a satellite—enough speed to escape Earth's gravity. After that initial blast, the rocket engine is discarded and the satellite coasts into orbit.

Project 6
STRAW ROCKET

As you learned in the previous activity, in order to launch a rocket you must first create a force. Try another way to use air under pressure to produce the force necessary to make a rocket fly.

Materials

modeling clay

2 plastic drinking straws, one slightly thinner than the other

2-liter soda bottle (empty and clean)

scissors

ruler

typing paper

transparent tape

Procedure

1. Wrap a piece of clay around one end of the thinner straw. Place the clay-covered end over the mouth of the soda bottle. Use the clay to seal the mouth.

2. Fill one end of the wider straw with a stopper made from a small amount of clay.

3. Cut two strips from the typing paper: a ½-by-3¼-inch (1.25-by-8-cm) strip and a ¾-by-4¾-inch (2-by-12-cm) strip.

4. Make a loop out of the shorter paper strip, overlapping the ends about 1 inch (2.5 cm). Tape the ends inside and outside the loop so that the overlapping ends form a narrow slit, about ½ inch

(1.25 cm) wide. Repeat with the longer paper strip.

5. Slide the open end of the wider straw into the slit in the smaller loop. Move the loop toward the end of the straw that has the clay stopper.

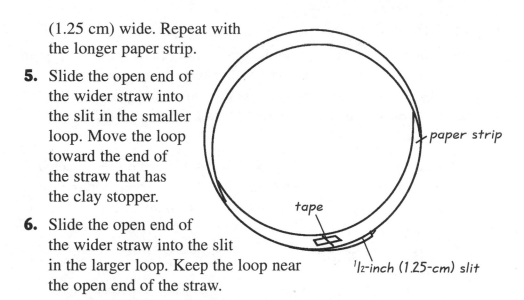

paper strip

tape

¹/₂-inch (1.25-cm) slit

6. Slide the open end of the wider straw into the slit in the larger loop. Keep the loop near the open end of the straw.

7. Tape the loops in place.

8. Place the wider straw over the straw attached to the bottle. Position the wider straw so that the loops are on the same side of the straw.

9. Squeeze the bottle with a sudden, forceful action. What happens?

CAUTION: Be sure to point the rocket away from people, including yourself.

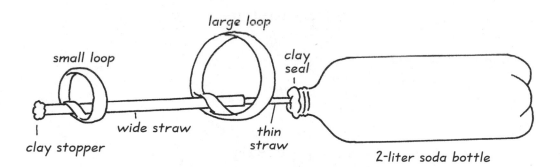

large loop

small loop

clay seal

wide straw

clay stopper

thin straw

2-liter soda bottle

MORE FUN STUFF TO DO

Repeat the activity, using different-size plastic bottles. Do certain bottles make the rocket fly better?

Explanation

When you squeeze the soda bottle, the air molecules are **compressed**, or pushed closer together, increasing the air pressure inside the bottle. (**Air pressure** is the force exerted by the movement of air molecules.) The air pressure creates a force that pushes out against the walls of the bottle in every direction.

The air also pushes against the opening where the straw is attached to the bottle. Newton's Third law of motion—for every action there is an equal and opposite reaction—then comes into play. The action is the air rushing out the opening. The reaction is the air pushing on the second straw with the paper loops, causing it to fly off rapidly.

Project 7
CHEMICAL LAUNCHER

Rockets don't actually use air pressure to launch into space; they use fuel. Try this activity to make your own "fuel" to launch a rocket.

Materials

four 1-by-12-inch (2.5-by-30-cm) paper streamers
cork to fit in the ½-gallon (2-liter) soda bottle
thumbtack
½ cup (125 ml) water
½ cup (125 ml) vinegar
2-liter soda bottle (empty and clean)
1 teaspoon (5 ml) baking soda
4-inch-square (10-cm) piece of paper towel

Procedure

NOTE: This activity must be performed outdoors with adult supervision.

CAUTION: Make sure that the cork is snug, but not too tight, when inserted into the mouth of the soda bottle. The cork must be loose enough to pop out when pressure is applied to the bottle.

1. Attach the four paper streamers to the end of the cork, using the thumbtack.

2. Place the water and vinegar in the bottle.

3. Place the baking soda in the center of the paper towel. Roll the paper towel into a tube and twist the ends of the tube to keep the baking soda inside.

4. Stand the bottle on the ground. Drop the paper tube into the bottle and insert the cork so that it is snug, but not too tight.

5. Move at least 10 feet (3 m) away. What happens?

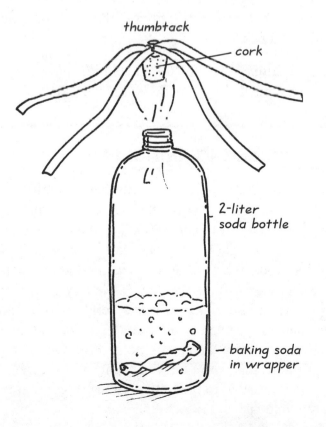

Try using different amounts of vinegar and baking soda. How can you make the cork rocket go the highest distance possible?

Explanation

The water-and-vinegar mixture slowly soaks through the paper towel. When the baking soda and vinegar mix together, a chemical reaction occurs. A **chemical reaction** is a change in matter in which substances break apart to produce one or more new substances. One new substance formed in this chemical reaction is **carbon dioxide** (the gas we naturally breathe out).

More and more carbon dioxide forms inside the bottle, taking up space. There is less room for the moving air molecules in the bottle, and the air pressure in the bottle increases. The air molecules push in all directions, including on the bottom of the cork. When the air pressure inside the bottle becomes greater than the force holding the cork, the cork launches.

The chemical reactions that launch rockets into space are much more powerful than the reaction that made your rocket fuel. In some rockets

COSMIC SCIENCE IN ACTION

Modern rocketry began with Russian schoolteacher Konstantin Tsiolkovsky (1857–1935), who published a paper on space travel in 1903. The American engineer Robert Goddard (1882–1945), however, was the founder of U.S. rocketry. In 1926, he became the first person to launch a liquid-fueled rocket. Fueled by gasoline and liquid oxygen, the rocket rose to a height of 41 feet (12.5 m), reached a top speed of 60 mph (97 kph), and landed 184 feet (56 m) from the launch point. Although few people realized it, this was a turning point in history. It would soon be possible to break the hold of Earth's gravity and travel into space.

a mixture of liquid hydrogen and liquid oxygen is burned to create a very powerful chemical reaction. This chemical reaction releases hot gases that rush out the engine nozzle, **propelling** (moving forward) a rocket into space.

Project 8
REENTRY

The first astronauts traveled in space capsules launched into orbit by rockets. NASA engineers not only had to put the astronauts and the space capsule into orbit, but also had to bring them back to Earth. In order to land, the capsule had to be slowed down just before reaching Earth's surface. Try the following activity to learn one way this was done.

Materials

small plastic toy

12-inch-square (30-cm) piece of plastic wrap

five 12-inch-long (30-cm) pieces of string

Procedure

1. Drop the toy from a high place, such as the top of a stairwell. How quickly does it fall?

CAUTION: Do not stand anywhere that does not have a handrail to hold on to.

2. Lay the piece of plastic wrap flat on a table.

3. Using four pieces of string, tie one end of each string to each corner of the plastic wrap.

4. Bring the other ends of the strings together and tie the ends in a knot.

5. Tie one end of the fifth piece of string to the plastic toy. Tie the other end to the knotted strings so that the toy has a parachute.

6. Repeat step 1 with your toy and parachute. Now how quickly does the toy fall to the ground?

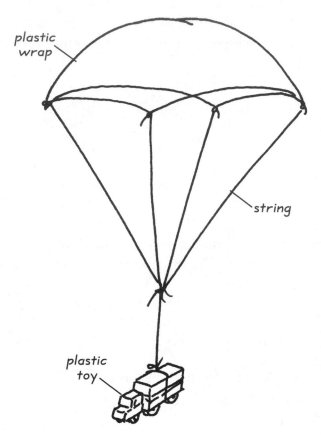

plastic
wrap

string

plastic
toy

MORE FUN STUFF TO DO

1 Try making parachutes with different materials, such as cloth, tissues, and the like. Which material works best?

2 Try different sizes and shapes of parachutes. Make them larger, smaller, round, oval, and rectangular. Which size and shape work best?

3 Try different sizes of plastic toys. What happens with bigger toys?

Explanation

A **parachute** is an umbrella-shaped device that slows an object's fall from a great height, such as from an airplane. A parachute is affected by two forces: gravity pulling it down and air resistance opposing this movement. The pull of gravity is much greater than air resistance, so the air only slows the rate of falling. The larger the parachute, the more air resistance it meets and the slower it falls.

Early space flights used parachutes in their final descent. The parachutes slowed the fall of the space capsule so that it could land in the ocean without harming the astronauts inside. Parachutes are also used to slow the speed of the space shuttle as it lands. When the space shuttle lands, it is moving too fast for its brakes alone to stop it, so it releases a series of parachutes behind it. The parachutes slow the space shuttle down enough for its brakes to stop it before it reaches the end of the runway.

COSMIC SCIENCE IN ACTION

Parachutes played an important role in NASA's *Galileo* space flight to Jupiter in 1996. The *Galileo* spacecraft flew within 600 miles (960 km) of Jupiter and released a **space probe**, a smaller, unmanned spacecraft that collects information. The pull of Jupiter's gravity increased the speed of the probe to 106,000 mph (170,000 kph). As the probe reached Jupiter's outer **atmosphere** (surrounding layer of gas), air resistance began to slow the probe's speed. At 200 miles (322 km) above the surface, the probe was traveling at 1,900 mph (3,000 kph). It released an 8-foot (2.4-m) parachute to slow it even farther. This slower speed allowed the probe to record and send back new information about Jupiter.

During the probe's 57-minute transmission, it descended 97 miles (156 km). New information received from the probe has provided scientists with new data to develop new theories about Jupiter and how our solar system's planets were formed.

Up There!
Orbiting Earth

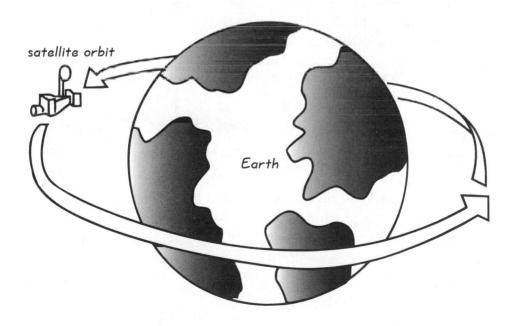

satellite orbit

Earth

The first satellites and space capsules launched into space orbited Earth. But what does it actually mean to orbit Earth?

In the 1600s, Isaac Newton first imagined that it would be possible to put an object into orbit around Earth. Newton imagined putting a great amount of gunpowder into a cannon. The cannon would shoot out the cannonball at a very high speed. The cannonball would travel so fast that as it fell back to Earth, the planet would curve away from the cannonball. The cannonball would continue to fall back to Earth, only to have Earth continually curve away from it. The cannonball would be in orbit around Earth.

An object orbits Earth because it is moving at just the right speed above Earth's surface. Gravity tries to pull the object back to Earth, but the object is moving so fast that as it falls, Earth curves away.

Any object in space that orbits something else is a satellite. The Moon is a natural satellite of Earth. However, there are many man-made satellites orbiting Earth as well. The first man-made satellite to orbit Earth was called *Sputnik I*, and it was launched in 1957.

Today there are over 200 working satellites in orbit around Earth. These satellites perform different tasks, like providing us with instantaneous phone calls and allowing us to watch on TV events happening around the world.

Try the following activities to learn more about orbiting Earth.

Project 1
FREE FALL

On the surface of Earth, all objects are affected by the force of gravity. But what happens to objects in orbit? Are they still affected by the force of gravity? Are they weightless? Try the following activity to find out.

Materials

bucket
pencil
paper cup
pitcher of tap water
yardstick (meterstick)

Procedure

NOTE: Perform this activity outdoors or cover your workspace to protect it from splashing water.

1. Place the bucket on the floor.

2. Use the pencil to make a hole in one side of the paper cup near the bottom.

3. Place your finger over the hole. Use the pitcher to fill the cup with water, keeping your finger over the hole.

4. Hold the cup upright about 3 feet (1 m) over the bucket. Remove your finger. What happens?

5. Place your finger back over the hole and refill the cup with water.

6. Again hold the cup upright about 3 feet (1 m) over the bucket. This time remove your finger from the hole, then drop the cup. What happens?

43

Explanation

Gravity pulls on all objects near the surface of Earth. In this activity, when you remove your finger from the hole in the cup, gravity pulls on the water, causing it to flow out of the hole. Gravity pulls on the water while your hand holds the cup in place. However, when you let the cup go, the cup falls at the same speed as the water. The same force of gravity is acting on both the cup and the water, so the water doesn't flow out of the cup. The water is weightless compared to the cup, because they both have the same force acting on them.

Like the water and the cup, objects that orbit Earth are falling. Gravity still pulls on objects in orbit. However, it pulls equally on both a spacecraft and the objects in the spacecraft, and the objects in it seem weightless.

Project 2
JUMPING COINS

Astronauts in orbit around Earth experience weightlessness. But are they really weightless? Try the following activity to find out.

Materials

pencil
8-ounce (250-ml) paper cup
2 rubber bands, each 2¼ inches (5.5 cm) long
small paper clip
tape
2 coins or metal washers

Procedure

1. Use the pencil to make a small hole in the center of the bottom of the paper cup.

2. Hook the rubber bands onto the paper clip as shown.

3. From the inside of the cup, push the paper clip through the hole in the cup, keeping the ends of the rubber bands inside the cup. Spread the paper clip apart on the outside of the cup so that it cannot be pulled back through the hole.

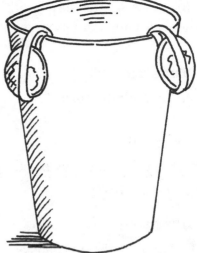

4. Pull each rubber band so that it is at its longest length without stretching. Tape a coin to the free end of each rubber band so that the coins rest just outside the cup. (Do not tape the rubber bands or the coins to the cup.)

5. Hold the cup upright at eye level. Drop the cup and allow it to fall. What happens?

Explanation

When you drop the cup, the coins are pulled into the cup. Before you drop the cup, the coins are held in place outside the cup because of two forces acting equally on them: the force of gravity pulling the coins down and the force of the elastic band pulling the coins into the cup. Because both forces are equal, the coins stay where they are.

However, when the cup begins to fall, both the coins and the cup are accelerated by gravity. The coins have the same acceleration as the cup, creating the effect of no gravity. The only force left to act on the coins is the force of the rubber bands, which pulls the coins into the cup as the cup falls.

Astronauts in orbit around Earth experience an apparent weightlessness, as do all falling objects. The astronauts are actually falling around Earth at the same rate as their shuttlecraft, which creates the effect of weightlessness.

Project 3
SPINNING IN ORBIT

How do satellites stay in orbit? Why don't they fall back to Earth? Try the following activity to learn why they stay in orbit.

Materials

plastic ballpoint pen
1-yard (1-m) piece of string
tennis ball
rock about same size as ball
masking tape

Procedure

1. Remove the end caps and ink cartridge from the pen and set them aside.

2. Thread the string through the empty pen tube.

3. Tie the tennis ball to one end of the string and the rock to the other. Wrap the tape several times over the string around the ball and the rock to secure the string.

string

tennis ball

pen tube

rock

4. Hold the rock in one hand and the pen tube in the other so that the pen tube is upright over the rock and about half the string is between your hands. Raise your arms above your head and begin to spin the ball in a horizontal circle by moving the pen tube in a circle.

5. Release the rock and allow it to hang freely. Observe what happens.

FUN STUFF TO DO

Try spinning the ball faster and then slower. What happens to the rock?

Explanation

According to the law of inertia, the moving ball will go in a straight line, unless acted on by an outside force. Whenever you move an object in a circle, a force pulls it inward to the center of the circle. This force is called **centripetal force**. Centripetal force changes the direction of your spinning ball, so it goes in a circle and not in a straight line.

If you were to let go of the pen tube, the centripetal force would be removed, and the ball would fly off in a straight line. The ball would also fly off in a straight line if you removed the rock.

The force of gravity also comes into play in this activity. The force of gravity pulls the rock down, which pulls on the string and ball.

These are the same forces that keep an object in orbit around Earth. Gravity provides a centripetal force that makes an object move in a circle rather than fly off into space. The object must be going fast enough to balance the force of gravity. If the object does not go fast enough, it will fall back to Earth. If the object goes too fast, it will orbit in larger and larger circles, eventually leaving orbit and traveling in space.

Project 4
STABLE SPINNING

In the last activity, you saw how objects in orbit move in circles. Try the next activity to learn more about moving in circles in space.

Materials

24-inch (60-cm) piece of string
LP phonograph record
toothpick

Procedure

1. Thread the string through the center of the record.

2. Tie one end of the string to the center of the toothpick. Pull the string through the record until the toothpick is tight against the underside of the record.

3. Holding the other end of the string, use the string to swing the record in a circle in front of you. How does the record move?

4. Use your free hand to spin the record on the string, then use the string to swing the spinning record in a circle. How does the record move now?

Explanation

When you first use the string to spin the record, the record wobbles as you swing it. However, when you spin the record before you swing it, the spinning keeps the record spinning, even when you swing it. Like all moving objects, spinning objects follow Newton's first law, the law of inertia (objects in motion will stay in motion unless acted on by an outside force). Spinning objects will stay spinning unless acted on by an outside force.

Like the spinning record, a spinning object moving in an orbit is more stable than an object that doesn't spin. The planets in our solar system are stable because they **rotate** (turn or spin around a center point) on their axes as they **revolve** (move in a curved path or orbit) around the Sun.

Project 5
FLYING STRAIGHT

How do astronauts keep their spacecraft in orbit without going off course? Try the following activity to explore one way.

Materials

sheet of paper

pencil

nail

plastic lid, such as from a cottage cheese container
(clean and dry)

ruler

adult helper

Procedure

1. Place the sheet of paper on a table or other flat surface.

2. Hold the pencil upright with its point on the paper. Let go of the pencil. What happens?

3. Have an adult use the nail to make a small hole in the center of the plastic lid. Push the pencil through the hole so that the pencil point is about 1 inch (2.5 cm) past the lid.

4. Hold the pencil and lid upright with the pencil point on the paper. Let go of the pencil. What happens?

5. Hold the pencil and lid upright between your palms with the pencil point on the paper. Move your palms quickly in opposite directions, then release the pencil to make it spin on its point. What happens to the spinning pencil? What design does the spinning pencil create?

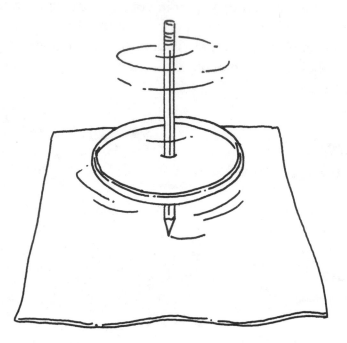

Explanation

When you first try to stand the pencil on its point, it falls over because of the pull of gravity. It also falls over with the plastic lid attached. However, when you spin the pencil with the lid attached, the pencil balances on its point. This is because a spinning object is more stable than an object that doesn't spin. This property is called the **gyroscopic effect**. The device you created is called a **gyroscope** (a wheel or disk mounted to spin rapidly about an axis).

A gyroscope is more stable than an object that doesn't spin. This stability increases with the mass and diameter of the object. (The **diameter** of an object is the distance between the endpoints of a line passing through the center of the object.) Adding the plastic lid increases the pencil's stability, making it easier for the pencil to spin on its point.

Friction and gravity are the outside forces that eventually stop the gyroscope from spinning. Friction between the pencil and paper slows it down, while gravity causes it to begin to tip over and draw circles.

Gyroscopes are used to **navigate** (steer a course for) both spacecraft and airplanes. The gyroscope is pointed in the direction that the astronaut or pilot wishes to travel and is kept spinning at a constant speed. If the aircraft moves off course, the change in direction creates an outside force. This force affects the gyroscope, which signals the autopilot to return the craft to its correct heading. (An **autopilot** is a device that steers a spacecraft or airplane automatically. The **heading** is the direction in which the spacecraft or airplane is going.) In space, computers continually monitor the gyroscope's data to keep the spacecraft on course.

Project 6
PLANTS IN ORBIT

Gravity causes plant stems and leaves to grow up and plant roots to grow down. So how would plants grow in space? Try the following activity to learn how.

Materials

newspaper

three 8-ounce (250-ml) paper cups

potting soil

6 bean seeds (from pack of planting seeds)

ruler

tap water

12 toothpicks

record player

masking tape

Procedure

NOTE: Ask an adult's permission to use the record player and keep it on for 3 weeks.

1. Cover your work area with newspaper.

2. Fill the paper cups with potting soil.

3. Place two bean seeds in each cup of soil. Push the seeds into the soil so that they are about ½ inch (1.25 cm) below the surface. Add a small amount of soil to make sure the seeds are covered.

4. Moisten the soil thoroughly with tap water. Pack the moist soil down in the cup with your hands.

5. Stick four toothpicks horizontally in a tick-tack-toe pattern through each paper cup at the surface level of the soil. (These toothpicks will help hold the soil in place during the activity.)

6. Locate a warm, sunny place where you can grow your plants undisturbed for 3 weeks. Cover the area with newspaper and set the record player there.

7. Place one cup right side up in the warm placc. Lay the second cup nearby on its side.

8. Lay the third cup on its side on the record player turntable so that the bottom of the cup is on the outer edge of the turntable and the top of the cup points toward the center. Tape the cup in place.

9. Turn on the record player to its slowest speed and keep it on.

10. Be sure to water all three containers each day. (The containers on their sides will have to be turned upright to water.) Observe the bean seeds each day for 3 weeks. What happens?

Explanation

The plants grown in the upright cup sprout, then grow straight up. The plants grown in the cup lying on its side sprout, then turn and begin to grow upright. They look as if they are growing sideways from the cup. The plants on the record player turntable also sprout. However, although they are lying on their side, they grow straight from the cup toward the center of the turntable.

Plants always grow upright because they feel the pull of gravity. The roots of a plant grow toward the pull of gravity, and the stem and leaves grow away from the pull of gravity. When the cup is upright, the roots grow down and the stem and leaves grow up out of the cup. When the cup is lying on its side, the roots still feel the pull of gravity and grow down. The stem and leaves still grow away from the pull of gravity, even though they must grow crooked.

However, when the seeds are put on the turntable, the force created by the turning is greater than the force of gravity. The plant reacts to the turning force as if it were the force of gravity. (This turning force, called **centrifugal force,** is the force that appears to push outward on a rotating body. Centrifugal force is actually inertia trying to make a moving object continue to move in a straight-line path.) The roots grow away from the centrifugal force, and the stem and leaves grow toward it.

To grow plants in space, scientists must create this type of artificial gravity. If the spacecraft spins while it moves, the spinning action will create this needed force. Scientists plan to build rotating space stations someday. (**Space stations** are large satellites orbiting Earth with room on board for people to work and live.) The rotation would create an artificial gravity for plants and people, which would make working conditions inside the station more like those on Earth.

COSMIC SCIENCE IN ACTION

For 5 years in the 1970s, the first American space station, *Skylab*, was in operation. In 1986, the Russian space station *Mir* was launched into orbit. At the present time, *Mir* has room for up to six crew members, and it has hosted both Russian and U.S. astronauts and scientists.

The U.S. space program is planning to launch a new space station before the year 2000. The new station will be the size of two football fields, have a permanent crew of six, and will orbit Earth once every 90 minutes at a distance of 200 miles (322 km) above Earth's surface.

Engineers from 14 countries are currently building parts of the new space station on Earth. Between 1997 and 2002, U.S. space shuttles or Russian launch vehicles will deliver the parts to space in 36 separate missions.

4

"Look, Ma, I'm Floating!"

Living and Working in Space

In 1961, Russian cosmonaut Yury Gagarin (1934–1968) became the first human to rocket into space and orbit Earth. Today, men and women travel into space and orbit around Earth several times a year.

Most astronauts travel in space for just a few days, but now some stay longer in space stations. In 1992, Russian cosmonaut Sergei Krikalex returned to Earth after spending the longest time a human has ever spent in space: 313 days.

Life in space is much different from life here on Earth. As you know, there is no effect of gravity in an orbiting spacecraft. Without gravity, the human body begins to change. Scientists are still studying the changes. To learn more about humans living and working in space, try the next activities.

Project 1
BIG *g*'s, LITTLE *g*'s

It's exciting to think about being launched into space. But how many of us will ever actually experience the forces that an astronaut feels as she lifts off and orbits? The term used to describe these forces is the *g*. The term *g* stands for gravity and is equal to the force exerted by Earth's gravity on an object at rest. On Earth, we feel 1 *g*, or one times the force of Earth's gravity. A force of 3 *g*'s means three times the force of Earth's gravity; 0 *g*'s, or zero gravity, means no gravity. In order to feel these *g*'s, all you have to do is visit an amusement park with a roller coaster. Try the next activity to learn how.

Materials

roller coaster ride

Procedure

1. As you ride the roller coaster, feel the forces that the ride creates. Note when you feel increased and decreased forces. They may push you into your seat or lift you off of it.

2. As you ride, answer the following questions:

   • Where do you feel the greatest force during the ride?

   • As you go up a hill, do you feel heavier, lighter, or your usual weight?

- As you go over the **crest** (highest point) of a hill, do you feel heavier, lighter, or your usual weight?

- As you go down a hill, do you feel heavier, lighter, or your usual weight?

- As you pass through the bottom of the hill, do you feel heavier, lighter, or your usual weight?

crest
of
hill

bottom of hill

MORE FUN STUFF TO DO

If the amusement park has a roller coaster that does a loop, try riding it. What forces do you feel upside down at the top of the loop?

Explanation

As a roller coaster goes up or down a hill, it goes either against the force of gravity or with the force of gravity. When the roller coaster goes up a hill, the coaster is going against the force of gravity. The ride creates an upward force while gravity tries to pull you down. The result is that you experience a strong force and feel heavier than usual.

At the crest of the hill, you feel the least force. When the roller coaster reaches the crest of the hill, the front of the train follows the tracks down the other side of the hill. Your body is still moving up the hill while the train has already started down the other side. Newton's first law of motion (the law of inertia) states that an object in motion will stay in motion unless acted on by an outside force. According to Newton's law, your body keeps moving up, even though front of the train is going down. This makes you feel lighter than usual. This feeling is similar to what astronauts feel when they are in orbit.

You continue to experience less force and feel lighter than usual going down the hill. As you move down the hill, the ride creates a downward force in the direction of gravity. You are actually falling down the hill.

COSMIC SCIENCE IN ACTION

NASA allows astronauts to experience weightlessness by putting them in conditions similar to a roller coaster. The astronauts are put aboard a KC-135 jet transport, which is a large cargo airplane. The transport flies upward, similar to a roller coaster going uphill. Once it reaches a high enough altitude, its flight path is similar to a roller coaster going over the crest of a hill. The plane then goes into a steep dive, causing the astronauts to be lifted out of their seats.

During the dive, the astronauts experience 30 seconds of weightlessness until the plane changes direction from the dive to level flight. The process is repeated several times so that the astronauts can get used to the feeling of zero gravity. In this training exercise, gravity is still there, but the astronauts fall at the rate that the plane flies in a power dive, which feels like weightlessness.

To simulate the forces an astronaut feels during takeoff, NASA uses acceleration sleds. Astronauts are seated on the sled in a simulated space capsule. The sled is then accelerated down a track, allowing the astronauts to feel the same forces as those they will encounter at takeoff.

You feel the greatest force at the bottom of the hill. Once the roller coaster reaches the bottom of the hill, it follows the tracks up the next hill. Again, because of Newton's law, your body is still moving down the hill while the train has already started up in the same direction. You feel a strong force as the train and gravity pull on you in opposite directions. This feeling is similar to what astronauts feel when a rocket takes off.

Project 2
WATER WORKOUT

When astronauts work in space, there is no gravity. Also, they must wear space suits because there is no oxygen. What problems does this cause? Try the next activity to find out.

Materials

several coins

nut and bolt

screwdriver

sink or bathtub

rubber gloves

Procedure

1. Place the coins, nut and bolt, and screwdriver on a table. Pick up each object. Did you have any problems picking them up?

2. Fill the sink with water. Place the objects in the water.

3. Put on the rubber gloves and try to pick up each object. Can you pick them up as easily as before?

4. Try to put the nut on the bolt underwater. Can you do it?

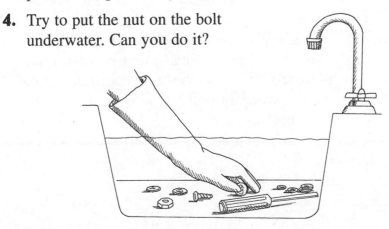

Go to a swimming pool with an adult. Have the adult watch you while you place several coins on the bottom of the pool. Put on a pair of rubber gloves and try to pick up each item.

COSMIC SCIENCE IN ACTION

To prepare astronauts for work in space, NASA has them work out in a swimming pool. They practice every action underwater that they will later perform in space.

NASA astronauts recently went on a space shuttle mission to repair the Hubble Space Telescope. The Hubble Space Telescope is a powerful, unmanned telescope that orbits Earth, allowing astronomers to view distant stars without the interference of Earth's atmosphere. After placing the telescope in orbit in 1990, NASA discovered a flaw in its design. Rather than bring Hubble back to Earth, NASA decided to repair it in space.

Before they went into space, the astronauts practiced their maneuvers in the NASA swimming pool. NASA placed exact models of the space shuttle loading bays and the Hubble Space Telescope underwater. (A **loading bay** is the part of the shuttle where cargo is carried.) The astronauts practiced catching the telescope, removing its outer coverings, and repairing it before releasing it into orbit again. Only when the astronauts could safely and properly execute their work on Earth (actually, underwater) could the mission proceed. The mission was successful, and the Hubble Space Telescope allows astronomers to see distant stars never seen before.

Explanation

Working in space while wearing a space suit creates several problems. Space suits carry oxygen supplies that allow astronauts to breathe, and they provide pressure on the astronauts' bodies that is normally provided by air. Space suits are very thick and bulky, which can make it difficult to work. The rubber gloves in this activity allow you to experience what it's like to work while wearing a space suit. You probably noticed that it's much more difficult to pick up small items while you are wearing the gloves.

Working without the effect of gravity is also difficult. Working underwater creates a situation similar to zero gravity. The water creates a **buoyant** (floating) force that tries to hold you up, decreasing the effect of gravity. As first it might seem easier to work without gravity. But gravity has an advantage: it holds you in place while you're working. In zero gravity, everything, including you, floats. Without gravity, you just might float away from where you want to be.

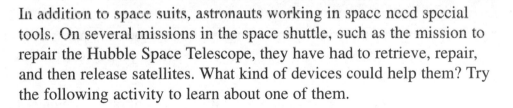

Project 3
ROBOT ARM

In addition to space suits, astronauts working in space need special tools. On several missions in the space shuttle, such as the mission to repair the Hubble Space Telescope, they have had to retrieve, repair, and then release satellites. What kind of devices could help them? Try the following activity to learn about one of them.

Materials

scissors

ruler

8½-by-11-inch (21.25-by-27.5-cm) piece of cardboard

nail

2 wire brads

wire coat hanger

pliers

2 paper clips

walnut-size ball of modeling clay

adult helper

Procedure

1. Cut three pieces of cardboard, each 11 × 2 inches (27.5 × 5 cm).

2. Have an adult use the nail to make a small hole in each end of each piece of cardboard. Center the holes about 1 inch (2.5 cm) from the end.

3. Line up the cardboard pieces as shown in the diagram, with the first hole of the second piece covering the second hole of the first piece, and the first hole of the third piece covering the second hole of the second piece.

4. Insert a brad in both pairs of overlapping holes. Bend back the ends of the brads to attach the cardboard pieces, but not so tightly that the pieces are unable to move.

5. Have an adult unbend and straighten the coat hanger and then use the pliers to make a small loop at one end of the wire.

6. Insert the wire loop through the second hole in the third piece of cardboard as shown.

7. Test the movement of the cardboard arm by holding on to the opposite end of the arm (piece ȴ) with one hand and moving the coat hanger wire with the other hand. Adjust the attachments until the arm moves freely.

8. Open one of the paper clips to make a hook. Hook the paper clip through the hole in the third piece of cardboard just below the coat hanger loop.

9. Push the other paper clip halfway into the ball of clay. The end of the paper clip should stick out to form a hook.

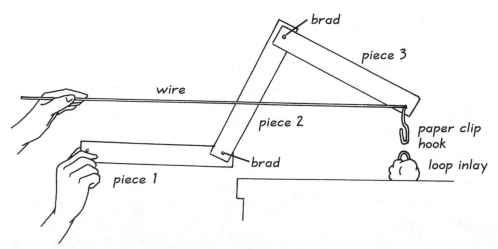

10. Place the clay ball on the table so that the hook points up. Hold the cardboard arm about 18 inches (45 cm) away from the clay ball.

11. Use the coat hanger wire to move the arm and pick up the clay ball. Can you do it? What problems do you have?

MORE FUN STUFF TO DO

1 Try putting the clay ball closer to you and farther away from you. In which location is it easier to retrieve the ball?

2 Design your own tool to do the same task. How else could you make this kind of device?

Explanation

The cardboard arm you made is a **simple machine** (a device that helps you to do work more easily) called a lever. A **lever** is made up of a rigid board or bar that is supported at a fixed point called a **fulcrum**. Actually, the cardboard arm is a series of levers. The cardboard pieces are the rigid boards, and the wire brads are the fulcrums. Levers make it easier to lift heavy loads because they magnify the force exerted; in other words, they turn a small force into a big one. Levers can also be used to move objects that are not near you. In this activity, the cardboard arm allows you to lift the clay ball when it's beyond your arm's reach.

The cardboard arm you made in this activity is a model of the robot arm that is routinely used on the space shuttle. Called the Canadarm, it was designed and built in Canada as part of the international cooperation of the current NASA space program.

Project 4
UPSIDE DOWN

Some tools we use every day can't be used in space. Try the following activity to see why.

Materials

2 sheets of typing paper
hardcover book
ballpoint pen
pencil
2 rubber bands

Procedure

1. Put one sheet of paper on the book. Use the pen and pencil to write different words.

2. Put the other sheet of paper on the book. Secure the paper to the book with the rubber bands. Lie on your back. With your arms outstretched, hold the book in front of you.

3. Use the pen and pencil again to write different words. How do the pen and pencil work when writing upside down?

Explanation

Ballpoint pens work because of the force of gravity. Gravity pulls ink from the ink cartridge onto a roller ball at the tip. The ink is rolled from the roller ball onto the paper. When you hold a ballpoint pen upside down, however, the ink can't flow onto the roller ball, and the pen won't write.

Pencil lead is actually graphite, a soft, black form of carbon found in nature. When the pencil point is rubbed against the paper, some of the graphite is left behind. Gravity does not affect how a pencil works.

COSMIC SCIENCE IN ACTION

In the early 1960s, when the U.S. manned space program was just beginning, NASA faced a serious problem. How would astronauts record information in space? At the time, all pens used gravity to work. NASA engineers had to invent a new type of pen that would work without gravity. After many unsuccessful tries, one young engineer came up with a way for astronauts to write in space. He suggested they use a pencil.

Project 5
EATING IN SPACE

Astronauts have to eat in space, but without gravity, can food move down from their mouths to their stomachs? Try the next activity to find out.

Materials

plastic drinking glass

plastic squeeze bottle with straw

water

horizontal bar at about eye level that can hold your weight
  (such as at a park or playground)

slice of bread

adult helper

Procedure

1. Fill the glass and squeeze bottle with water.

2. Hang upside down by your knees from the bar.

3. Have the adult hand you the bread. Eat the bread while upside down. What happens?

4. Have the adult hand you the glass of water. Drink water while hanging upside down. What happens?

5. Have the adult hand you the squeeze bottle. Drink water from the squeeze bottle. What happens?

MORE FUN STUFF TO DO

Eat other kinds of food, such as fruit, while upside down. How does gravity make eating food easier?

Explanation

Although it might have felt a little strange, you were able to eat and drink while hanging upside down. This is because gravity isn't necessary for food and liquids to move from your mouth to your stomach. When you swallow, food is forced into a tube called the **esophagus** that connects your mouth to your stomach. The walls of the esophagus automatically **contract** (squeeze together) and relax, which moves the food along the esophagus toward your stomach.

Gravity doesn't move food and drink from your mouth to your stomach, but without gravity, getting the food into your mouth in the first place can be difficult. As you saw with the glass of water, gravity makes it easier for water to flow into your mouth. However, a squeeze bottle makes it easy to both eat and drink in space.

Astronauts in the space shuttle mostly eat dried foods, adding water just before eating. They squeeze their mixing bags and the food goes right into their mouths. This method of eating works well, but the drying process makes the food rather tasteless. Also, many astronauts can't smell the food they're eating. Stuffed-up heads, a common problem in space, no doubt cause most of the problem. Astronauts have long complained that their diet is too bland. Most scientists say that the major reason is the lack of smell.

Project 6
INNER CONFUSION

Your inner ear helps your body know whether you are right side up or upside down. In other words, it helps you balance. Does your inner ear work in space without gravity? Try the following activity to learn more about your inner ear.

Materials

swivel chair

scarf that can be used as a blindfold

timer

helper

Procedure

1. Place the chair in the center of the room. Make sure you have enough space to turn the chair in circles without stopping.

2. Have your helper sit in the chair. Use the scarf to blindfold your helper then ask her to lift her feet off the floor.

3. Turn the chair slowly in one direction. Time the turns to make one complete turn every 2 to 3 seconds, turning at a constant speed. Ask your helper how she feels.

4. After 1 minute, stop turning the chair. Again ask your helper how she feels.

Explanation

When the chair first begins to spin, your helper should sense the turning motion. After about 30 seconds, however, she won't feel the turning at all. When you stop turning the chair after 1 minute, your helper will feel that she is turning in the opposite direction, even though she has stopped.

The canals of your inner ear are filled with fluid. The movement of the fluid sends messages of movement to your brain. When you first turn your helper, the fluid in the canals of her ear lags behind, then moves. The fluid doesn't move right away because of inertia (the tendency of an object to resist a change in motion). But as the spinning continues, the fluid flows in the direction of the spin. Your friend doesn't feel as if she is moving. When the chair stops turning, the fluid resists the stopping motion and incorrectly sends signals to your helper's brain that she's moving in the opposite direction.

The apparent weightlessness of being in orbit similarly affects an astronaut's inner ear. On Earth, even with your eyes closed, you know which direction down is because gravity pulls on the fluids in your inner ear. When an astronaut is in orbit, however, her inner ear is "confused," much as your helper's was in this activity. When an astronaut returns to Earth, she can't balance for a while. Eventually, however, her sense of balance comes back.

Project 7
GROWING TALL

Strange things can happen to the human body in space. Try the following activity to learn about one of them.

Materials

tape measure
pencil
notebook
helper

Procedure

1. Have a helper use the tape measure to measure your height at the end of the day just before you go to bed. Record your height.

2. Place the pencil next to your bed so that you will be able to reach it the next morning without sitting up.

3. The next morning when you wake up, do not sit up. Move to the end of the bed so that your heels are at the end of your mattress. Place the pencil on the bed at the top of your head.

4. Sit up without disturbing the pencil, and measure your height. Is your height the same as it was the night before?

Explanation

First thing in the morning, you are about ½ inch (1.25 cm) taller than you were the night before. This is because of the way your spine is made up. Your spine consists of 26 linked bones, called **vertebrae**. Between each pair of vertebrae is a flexible disk made of **cartilage**, a tough, elastic tissue, covering other, softer tissue. The disks act as shock absorbers for the body, compressing slightly when forces are applied to them.

The biggest force your body faces every day is gravity. Gravity compresses the disks in your back when you are standing or sitting. At night, when you are lying down, gravity does not compress the disks and they relax. The relaxed disks make you slightly taller in the morning. However, this gain in height quickly leaves once you stand up.

In space, where there is zero gravity, the effect is even more noticeable. With no gravity to compress the disks in the back for several days or even weeks, astronauts report that they've grown as much as 2 inches (5 cm) in space.

Project 8
BAD BONES

Astronauts who've spent long periods of time in space have found that once back on Earth, they're weak and even have a hard time standing up. What's the trouble? Try the following activity to find out.

Materials

bone from a cooked chicken (a drumstick works best)
glass jar
white vinegar
tap water
adult helper

Procedure

1. Ask an adult to remove as much of the meat as possible from the chicken bone and clean the bone when finished.

2. Try to bend the cleaned bone. Can you do it?

3. Place the chicken bone in the jar. Pour enough vinegar in the jar to completely cover the bone. (Don't put a lid on the jar.) Set the jar aside for 2 days.

4. Pour out the vinegar in the jar and replace it with the same amount of fresh vinegar. Set the jar aside for 2 more days. Repeat the process every 2 days for a total of 8 days.

5. Pour out the vinegar from the jar. Rinse the bone with water. Observe the chicken bone. Try to bend it. Can you bend it now?

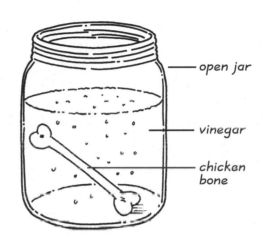

open jar

vinegar

chicken bone

Explanation

You should be able to bend the chicken bone after it has soaked in the vinegar for 8 days. Vinegar is an **acid**, a sour substance with special chemical properties. In this activity, the vinegar reacts chemically with a substance in the bone called calcium. **Calcium** is an important **mineral** (nonliving, naturally occurring substance) in the body that makes bones strong. The vinegar dissolves the calcium, removing it from the bone. The bone is no longer strong.

Actively using your body ensures that calcium stays in your bones. When the body isn't active, bones begin to lose calcium. The delicate balances in the human body are upset by the zero-gravity environment in space travel. Without gravity to work against, bones lose mass and calcium during long time periods in space.

Human bones in space would never lose all their calcium like the chicken bone. However, several Russian cosmonauts who spent many months in space returned to Earth only to find that their bones were barely strong enough to hold up their bodies in Earth's gravity. This effect eventually was reversed after the cosmonauts were back on Earth for a time. Today, cosmonauts and astronauts exercise every day in space to help ensure that their bones don't weaken.

5

Places We've Gone

Walking on the Moon

Can you believe that people have actually walked on the Moon? Our Moon is the closest object in space to Earth—much closer than Venus, the nearest planet. It's a logical place to visit, and in the late 1960s and early 1970s, NASA's Apollo astronauts did just that.

On July 20, 1969, Neil Armstrong (1930–) took, as he said, "one small step for man, one giant leap for mankind," when he became the first person to walk on the Moon. We had sent unmanned spacecraft to the Moon before, but this was the first time humans had set foot on a place in our solar system other than Earth. There was so much to learn and investigate!

Between 1969 and 1972, Apollo astronauts made six trips to the Moon. On the Moon, the astronauts studied the landscape, set up experiments, and collected rocks to take back home. To learn more about missions to the Moon, try the next activities.

Project 1
CRATERS

Some of the first things astronauts noticed on the Moon were all the craters on its surface. What are craters, and what could have caused them? Try the following activity to find out.

Materials

6-ounce (170-g) package of instant chocolate pudding
baking pan
rubber spatula or table knife
bag of chocolate chips
adult helper

Procedure

1. Have an adult make the chocolate pudding according to the instructions on the box.

2. Place the pudding in the baking pan. Smooth the surface of the pudding with the rubber spatula.

3. Drop a chocolate chip onto the surface of the pudding. What happens?

4. Throw a chocolate chip at the surface of the pudding. What happens?

5. Throw a small handful of chocolate chips at the surface of the pudding. What happens?

Explanation

When you throw chocolate chips at the pudding's surface you make small craters. **Craters** are bowl-shaped imprints formed by the impact of an object hitting a surface. Like pudding craters, the Moon's craters were also formed by solid objects hitting a surface. These objects, called **meteorites,** are particles of matter (usually rock or metal) from the solar system that strike a surface. For thousands of years, meteorites have bombarded the Moon, creating large craters with their impact.

Craters found on Earth's surface show that Earth, too, has been hit by large meteorites. The Moon's surface has been hit by many more meteorites than Earth's, however, because the Moon doesn't have an atmosphere. Most particles from space burn up when they come in contact with Earth's atmosphere. Space particles that burn up in Earth's atmosphere are called **meteors**. Meteors look like streaks of light. We see them often and call them **shooting stars**.

Project 2
LUNAR WALKER

Once on the Moon, astronauts needed to travel away from the spacecraft in order to collect samples. How did they do this? Walking could only take them so far. Try this activity to learn one way.

Materials

thread spool
rubber band about the same length as the spool
thumbtack
metal washer
toothpick or similar object

Procedure

1. Slip the rubber band through the hole in the thread spool so that it passes from one end of the spool to the other.

2. Attach one end of the rubber band to the spool with the thumbtack.

3. Slip the other end of the rubber band through the hole in the metal washer to make a loop in the end of the rubber band.

4. Put the toothpick through the loop in the rubber band.

5. Turn the toothpick to wind up the rubber band inside the spool.

6. Place the spool on a table or floor and let your lunar walker go! What happens?

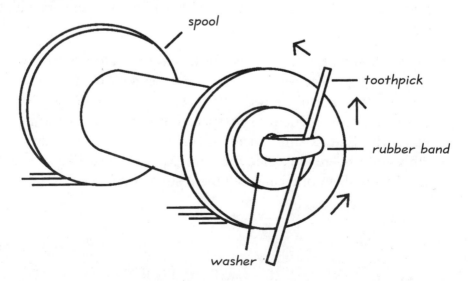

1 Try different-size spools and rubber bands on your lunar walker. Do they make the walker go faster or farther? Try other materials instead of the metal washer. Will a plastic washer work?

2 Try making your lunar walker move over different surfaces. For example, will it move over carpeting, grass, or soil? Can it go up and down hills?

Explanation

In this activity, you used energy to make the lunar walker move. **Energy** is the ability to do work. There are two main types of energy. **Kinetic energy** is the energy of moving objects. **Potential energy** is stored energy that has the ability to change into kinetic energy.

One kind of potential energy is **elastic energy**. Elastic energy is the energy stored in an object when its shape is changed by either **stretching** (pulling apart) or compressing (pushing together). A stretched rubber band and a coiled spring both have stored elastic energy. Stored elastic energy is released when the object is allowed to return to its natural shape.

Energy is never used up; it is just converted from one form to another. In this activity, stored elastic energy is **converted** (changed) into kinetic energy. You store energy by twisting the rubber band. When you release the rubber band, elastic energy is converted to kinetic energy, and the walker moves.

Of course, the "lunar walker" used by the Apollo astronauts wasn't powered by a rubber band. Potential energy stored in the vehicle's batteries was converted into kinetic energy when the vehicle moved. Like your lunar walker, when the astronaut's vehicle used up all the potential energy, it couldn't drive any farther. The astronauts carefully planned each trip so that the batteries wouldn't run out.

COSMIC SCIENCE IN ACTION

For the Apollo trips to the Moon, NASA designed a vehicle to allow the astronauts to travel a short distance on the Moon's surface. Gas could not be used, because a gas engine needs oxygen to run and there is no oxygen on the Moon. NASA engineers designed a vehicle that ran on electricity, called the Lunar Rover.

The Lunar Rover was like an open jeep powered by batteries. The Apollo astronauts took it with them on the last three trips to the Moon. The Lunar Rover only traveled at a maximum speed of 8¾ mph (14 kph), but it took the astronauts farther than they had gone before. On the last visit the Lunar Rover traveled nearly 21 miles (34 km).

Project 3
HOW HIGH?

How do astronauts walk on the Moon without floating away? Is there gravity on the Moon? Try the following activity to find out.

Materials

3-foot (1-m) piece of string

tape measure

helper

Procedure

NOTE: This activity must be performed in a large outdoor area.

1. Lay the string in a straight line on the ground. The string will be your starting line. There should be at least 10 feet (3 m) of open area beyond the string.

2. Stand with your toes just behind the string. Bend your knees, swing your arms, and jump as far as you can.

3. Remain standing where you landed, and have your helper use the tape measure to measure the distance from the string to the heel of your foot. How far did you jump?

4. Multiply the distance you jumped by 6. This is the distance you would be able to jump on the Moon.

MORE FUN STUFF TO DO

Repeat the activity with a vertical jump. Standing next to a wall, reach as far up the wall as you can. Mark the spot you reach with a piece of chalk. Holding the chalk in your hand, jump as high as you can and put another mark on the wall. Measure the distance between the two marks to determine your vertical jump on Earth. Multiply the distance by 6 to find out how high you could jump on the Moon. (Imagine a basketball game played on the Moon!)

Explanation

Gravity is the force that pulls *all* objects together, thus the Moon does have gravity. The force of gravity depends on the distance between objects and their masses. The greater the mass of an object, the greater its pull of gravity. The Moon has one-sixth the mass of Earth. Thus it has only one-sixth the pull of gravity that Earth does. You can jump six times higher and six times farther on the Moon than on Earth. If the Olympics were held on the Moon, athletes could perform better, but they'd have to compete wearing space suits.

Project 4
LOST ON THE MOON

Imagine it's 20 years in the future. You are a member of a crew scheduled to land at a science research station located on the lighted surface of the Moon. Because of an energy failure, you and the rest of the crew had to crash-land 125 miles (200 km) from the research station. During reentry and landing, much of the equipment aboard was damaged. Fifteen items of equipment were left undamaged. Since survival depends upon reaching the research station as soon as possible, you can only take the most critical items for the trip. What would you do? How can you make it to the research station? Try the following activity and see whether you would survive.

Materials

pencil

paper

Procedure

1. Copy the 15 items listed below on the sheet of paper.

2. Rank the items in terms of their importance in allowing your crew to reach the rendezvous point. Place a 1 next to the most important item, a 2 next to the second most important item, and so on up to 15, the least important item.

Salvaged Items from the Crashed Ship

- box of matches
- dried food
- parachute silk
- solar-powered portable heater
- 50 feet (15 m) of nylon rope
- solar-powered radio receiver-transmitter
- case of dried milk
- self-inflatable life raft
- magnetic compass
- 5 gallons (22.5 liters) water
- chemical signal flares
- first-aid kit
- two .45-caliber pistols
- two 100-pound (45-kg) tanks of oxygen
- star map

MORE FUN STUFF TO DO

1 Gather a group of friends together to see what group answer you come up with. Did the group's answer differ from the one you came up with personally?

2 Compare your answers with those from a group of NASA engineers. How well would you survive?

Explanation

A group of engineers from NASA were given the "Lost on the Moon" survival activity, and they ranked the items as follows:

1. two 100-pound (45-kg) tanks of oxygen

2. star map

3. 5 gallons (22.5 liters) water

4. solar-powered radio receiver-transmitter

5. chemical signal flares

6. parachute silk

7. 50 feet (15 m) of nylon rope

8. first-aid kit

9. dried food

10. two .45-caliber pistols

11. self-inflatable life raft

12. case of dried milk

13. solar-powered portable heater

14. magnetic compass

15. box of matches

The NASA engineers felt that the most important items for survival were oxygen, a map of the stars in the Moon's sky, water, and a radio receiver-transmitter. The Moon doesn't have an atmosphere like Earth does. There is no oxygen on the Moon, so astronauts must have a continuous supply of oxygen in order to survive. After oxygen, the next most important item is a star map. In a survival situation, the astronauts would need to know in which direction to travel to reach the science research station. A map of the Moon's sky helps the astronauts find their way.

Next the astronauts would need water, as there is no water on the Moon. The human body can go about 2 weeks without food but will last only a few days without water. The receiver-transmitter would allow the astronauts to contact the science research station when they got closer. The research station could then send out a rescue team.

The next items are less critical for survival. Flares, parachute silk, and nylon rope would all be useful, but the astronauts would not need them to survive. Food would also not be critical because the astronauts would use all their oxygen before they needed food.

The least important items for survival are matches and the magnetic compass. Without oxygen, the matches would be useless. The Moon does not have a magnetic field like Earth does, so the compass would not work either.

COSMIC SCIENCE IN ACTION

Every space mission has not gone perfectly. Two days after the *Apollo 13* spacecraft was launched on April 11, 1970, an oxygen tank exploded near its main engine. This explosion crippled the spacecraft's power and life-support systems and forced NASA to cancel the planned landing on the Moon.

The *Apollo 13* astronauts—James Lovell, Fred Haise, and John Swigert—used the engines of the lunar module (the part of the spacecraft that was to make the trip down to the Moon's surface) to speed the crippled spacecraft around the Moon and back to Earth. *Apollo 13* landed safely on Earth on April 17, 1970.

Places We'd Like to Go

Probing the Planets

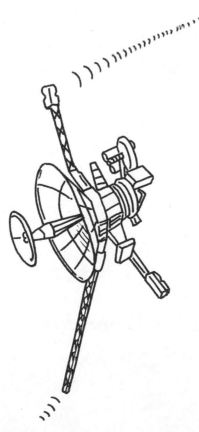

Humans have orbited Earth and gone to the Moon. So far, that's as far as we've traveled in space. But we have sent unmanned space probes to explore where we haven't gone.

Space probes are actually robots sent to investigate space and report back to Earth. The probes are launched into space to follow a prearranged route. A probe might be sent to orbit around or even land on a planet. Instruments on board gather information and send it back to Earth by radio.

We've already learned much about the solar system through probes. The first successful space probe, *Luna 2*, was sent to the Moon in 1959. *Viking 1* and *2* landed on Mars in 1976. In 1977 *Voyager 1* and *2* were launched to explore Jupiter, Saturn, Uranus, and Neptune. Through these probes we've explored our solar system without ever leaving Earth.

To learn more about probing the planets in our solar system, try the following activities.

Project 1
GRAVITY BOOST

It's a long way to travel from Earth to Saturn. How can a space probe use the planets to change its direction and increase its speed? Try the following activity to learn how.

Materials

2 hardcover books (same thickness)
ruler
12-inch-square (30-cm) piece of cardboard
metal ball the size of a marble
strong horseshoe magnet
12-inch (30-cm) piece of string

Procedure

1. Place the books flat on the table about 6 inches (15 cm) apart.

2. Lay the cardboard on top of the books to create a flat surface.

3. Roll the metal ball across the center of the cardboard. What happens?

4. Remove the cardboard. Place the magnet between the books, but slightly off center.

5. Replace the cardboard on top of the books.

6. Again roll the metal ball slowly across the center of the cardboard. What happens?

7. Remove the magnet and tie the string to it.

8. Put the magnet back in its original position.

9. Roll the metal ball slowly across the center of the cardboard, but this time as you do, pull the string on the magnet in the general direction that the ball rolls. What happens?

Explanation

In the first case, the metal ball rolls straight across the cardboard. The only force acting on it is your push. In the second case, the path of the metal ball curves toward the magnet. In the third case, the metal ball curves and changes direction due to the **magnetic force**, and it speeds up as you pull the magnet. (Magnetic force is the attracting or repelling force between a magnet and certain metals or other magnetic substances.)

The third case demonstrates what happens when a space probe travels near another planet. The force of a planet's gravity affects a probe the way the magnet affects the metal ball. As the probe passes a planet, the planet's gravity attracts the probe, causing it to change direction. Because the planet is orbiting the Sun, it pulls the probe along, transferring some of its speed to the probe. The probe is able to use the planet to change its direction and increase its speed. This technique is known as a **gravity assist** or **gravity boost.**

COSMIC SCIENCE IN ACTION

In 1977, the *Voyager 2* space probe was launched for a grand tour of Jupiter, Saturn, Uranus, and Neptune. Mission navigators used the gravity assists from these planets to provide extra speed and to change the direction of the probe. *Voyager* probably would never have made it to Saturn without a gravity boost from Jupiter. It would never have made it to Uranus and Neptune without a boost from Saturn. Each planet it visited speeded *Voyager* on its way to the next one.

Project 2
GETTING TO MARS

There are many ways for a space probe to go from Earth to Mars. While traveling in a straight line seems the easiest way, it requires more energy to power the launch rocket than we currently can supply. Try the next activity to learn the most energy-efficient way for a probe to travel in our solar system.

Materials

transparent tape
8½-by-11-inch (21.25-by-27.5-cm) sheet of typing paper
corkboard or cardboard
pencil
ruler
2 pushpins
12-inch (30-cm) piece of string

Procedure

1. Tape the paper to the corkboard.

2. Draw a horizontal line 3 inches (7.5 cm) long in the middle of the paper. Make a small pencil mark in the center of the line, 1½ inches (3.75 cm) from each side.

3. Make two pencil marks, each ¾ inch (2 cm) from the left and right of the center mark.

4. Make a pencil mark at each end of the horizontal line.

5. Stick the pushpins into the ¾-inch (2-cm) marks.

6. Tie the ends of the string together to make a loop. Loop the string over the ends of the pushpins.

7. Place the pencil point against the inside of the loop. Keep the string taut as you guide the pencil around the inside of the loop to draw an ellipse (oval).

8. Move the pins to the end marks. Repeat step 7 to draw a second ellipse.

9. Move the pin on the right to the ¾-inch (2-cm) mark, and keep the pin on the left at the end mark. Again, repeat step 7 to draw a third ellipse. What do you notice?

10. Make a pea-size dot at each place where the ellipses touch. Label the dot on the left MARS and the dot on the right EARTH.

11. Draw a circle the size of a quarter around the center mark. Label the circle the SUN.

Explanation

In this activity you drew three ellipses. The larger, outer ellipse represents the orbit of Mars. The smaller, inner ellipse represents the orbit of Earth. The ellipse that goes between the orbits of Mars and Earth represents the orbit that is the best way to travel between the two planets. This orbit is called a **transfer orbit**.

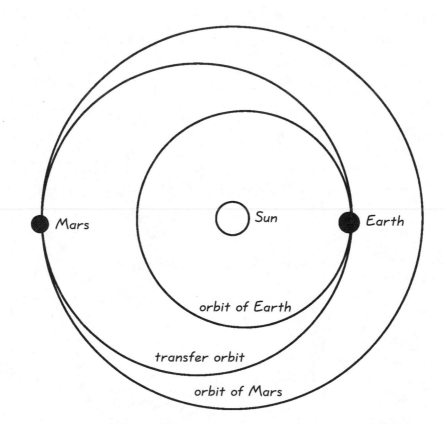

Launching a space probe in a transfer orbit is the most energy-efficient way for it to travel between planets. The probe is put into a transfer orbit around the Sun. In this activity, the transfer orbit is a semi-elliptical (half an oval) orbit that touches both Earth's orbit and Mars's orbit. The probe orbits the Sun, pulled along by the Sun's gravity. This transfer orbit was used in 1976 when NASA sent *Viking 1* and *2* to Mars.

Project 3
ARRIVING ON TIME

In the last activity, you learned how space probes travel in a transfer orbit from one planet to another. But the orbital pathway is only part of the problem. The trip must be timed so that the probe arrives at the planet. Try the next activity to understand the problem and learn about the solutions.

Materials

30 to 40 rocks
tape measure
3 sheets of paper
marking pen
2 helpers

Procedure

NOTE: This activity must be performed in a large, clear, flat outdoor area.

1. Place a rock in the center of the outdoor area. This rock represents the Sun.

2. Use the tape measure to measure a straight line about 25 yards (23 m) from the center rock. Place a second rock at that location.

3. Walk in a circle, staying about 25 yards (23 m) from the center rock. Mark the circle by putting a rock down about every 5 to 10 steps. This circle represents Mars's orbit.

4. Use the tape measure to measure a second straight line about 15 yards (14 m) from the center rock. Place a rock in that location. Walk in a circle, staying about 15 yards (14 m) from the center rock. Mark the circle by putting down a rock about every 5 to 10 steps. This circle represents Earth's orbit.

5. Write SUN on the first sheet of paper. Write EARTH on the second sheet and MARS on the third.

6. Place the Sun paper on the center rock. Let one helper hold the Earth paper and stand on the inner circle and the other helper hold the Mars paper and stand on the outer circle.

7. Have your helpers begin to walk in the same counterclockwise direction around their circles at a steady speed.

8. Walk next to the Earth helper. You represent a probe going to Mars.

9. At any time you choose, break away from "Earth" and begin jogging along a curved path toward "Mars." When you break away from Earth, look at the ground and keep moving at the same speed. Do not look up. Are you able to reach Mars?

MORE FUN STUFF TO DO

Repeat steps 6 through 9 until you are able to reach Mars. Let each helper take a turn being the space probe.

Explanation

In order to reach Mars, Mars must be slightly ahead of you when you break from Earth. Because Mars travels in a larger orbit, it travels a longer distance in one orbit compared to the orbit of Earth or the space probe. To make up for this difference, you must break from Earth when Mars is slightly ahead of you. Then, if you and Mars travel at about the same speed, your paths will meet each other at the same time.

For a real space probe to reach Mars using a transfer orbit, the probe must be launched when Mars is in just the right position. This position is called an **opportunity**. For Mars, an opportunity comes when Mars is 45° ahead of Earth in orbit as shown. This opportunity only comes about every 780 days.

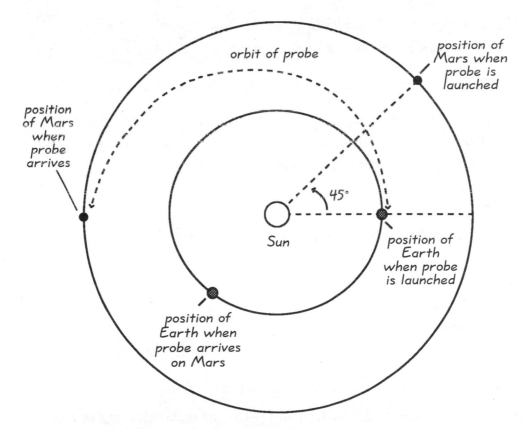

There is a different launch opportunity for each planet in the solar system. The time between launch opportunities varies for each planet. There are 116 days between launch opportunities to Mercury, 583 days between launch opportunities to Venus, and 398 days between launch opportunities to Jupiter.

COSMIC SCIENCE IN ACTION

The launch opportunity for NASA's *Voyager 2* in 1977 was a rare one indeed. The *Voyager 2* space probe was scheduled to visit Jupiter, Saturn, Uranus, and Neptune. The launch opportunity needed not only Mars to be in the correct position but the other four planets as well. That launch opportunity happens only once every 187 years. We will have to wait until the year 2164 to have another chance to make the flight.

Project 4
POSTCARDS FROM ANOTHER PLANET

Although humans have never traveled to other planets, space probes have told us a lot about what they are like. Imagine you could visit another planet. What would it be like writing to friends on Earth? What would you write? Try this activity to see what a postcard home might reveal about another planet.

Materials

astronomy book or encyclopedia

pencil

ruler

sheet of typing paper

crayons or markers

Procedure

1. Read about your favorite planet in the reference book.

2. Draw two 3½-by-6-inch (8.75-by-15-cm) rectangles on the paper. Draw a 3½-inch (8.75-cm) line on one of the rectangles, dividing the rectangle in half. These rectangles are the two sides of your postcard.

3. Pretend that you are visiting your favorite planet. Use the right half of the divided rectangle to address your postcard. Use the left half

to write a short message about your stay, which should give some information about the planet. For example, you could write, "We couldn't land on Saturn because it's a spinning ball of liquid. We landed on its biggest moon, Titan. The view of Saturn was terrific! Wish you could see it, too!"

4. On the undivided rectangle, use pencil and crayons to draw your planet.

Explanation

Someday humans may be able to travel to other planets. Each planet will pose its own problems. Jupiter and Saturn are balls of liquid. Uranus is also mostly liquid and gas, but it is smaller and very cold. Neptune and Pluto are solid but icy cold. Venus is extremely hot. The heat and the pressure from Venus's atmosphere would destroy a spacecraft. Mercury is extremely hot on the side facing the Sun but extremely cold on its dark side, as it has no atmosphere.

Mars is the most likely planet for humans to visit. Some scientists believe we could travel to Mars in the next century. Mars is very cold and has weaker gravity than that of Earth. The atmosphere on Mars contains large amounts of carbon dioxide, the gas we naturally breathe out, and there is no water. If we do visit Mars, we will have to wear space suits to allow us to breathe and protect us from the cold.

Living conditions would be difficult. And the trip to get there would take a long time. When Mars and Earth are closest, they are still 35 million miles (56 million km) apart.

COSMIC SCIENCE IN ACTION

The two Viking space probes that landed on Mars in the summer of 1976 gave us lots of information. They analyzed the soil and found it contains high amounts of the mineral iron. They searched for life on Mars but found none. The probes gave us a close-up view of the landscape of Mars. There are gigantic volcanoes. Olympus Mons is 435 miles (700 km) across and 17 miles (27 km) high, about three times as high as Mount Everest on Earth. There is also an enormous set of canyons, called the Valles Marineris, that is ten times longer and four times deeper than the Grand Canyon in Arizona. The soil and rocks are red, which is why Mars is sometimes called the Red Planet.

Even Farther

Seeing the Stars and More

lthough we may someday visit Mars, it's hard to imagine we'll ever visit a star. But there's a lot you can learn about stars right here from Earth.

Have you ever sat in the park after playing all day? As evening comes and the cool breeze starts, you may look up to see that the stars are beginning to come out. They've actually been there all the time, but it's not until night that we can see them.

There is one star that's visible during the day. It's the Sun, of course. It's the nearest star to Earth, just 93 million miles (150 million km) away. Without light and heat from the Sun, life on Earth as we know it could not exist.

But what about other stars? Do other stars provide the conditions for life on planets near them as well? What are shooting stars? Try the activities in this chapter to learn about the stars and more.

Project 1
COLD COMET

Have you ever seen something in the sky that looks like a star with a tail? Long ago people thought such sights were warnings of disaster. They're not bad omens, and they're not even stars; they're comets. But what are comets? Try the following activity to find out.

Materials

12 ounces (355 ml) club soda

large bowl

1 teaspoon (5 ml) sand

rubber gloves

1 teaspoon (5 ml) ammonia

mixing spoon

timer

warm tap water

adult helper

cookie sheet

Procedure

CAUTION: Use rubber gloves and handle ammonia with care. Adult supervision is required for this activity.

1. Pour the club soda into the bowl.

2. Add the sand. Put on the rubber gloves, then have the adult watch as you add the ammonia. Mix thoroughly with the spoon.

3. Place the mixture in the freezer until frozen solid. This will probably take about 2 hours.

4. Remove the frozen mixture from the freezer. Place the bottom of the bowl in warm running tap water until the frozen mixture unsticks from the bowl.

5. Place the frozen mixture on the cookie sheet. What does it look like?

rubber gloves

Explanation

Although comets may look like stars in the sky, they're actually more like giant dirty snowballs. **Comets** are actually icy lumps, which scientists believe come from a giant cloud near the edge of our solar system. Sometimes these comets get knocked off course and head toward the Sun.

The main part of a comet is its center, called its **nucleus**. A comet's nucleus is basically round and is a few miles (kilometers) wide. Most astronomers think a comet's nucleus consists of water, carbon dioxide gas, ammonia, dust, and small amounts of **methane**, commonly called natural gas. The frozen mixture that you made in this activity consists of club soda (which is basically water and carbon dioxide gas), ammonia, and sand. Your comet contains almost all the ingredients of a real comet.

But why does a comet seem so bright when we see one in the sky? When the comet moves closer to the Sun, it melts and forms a cloud of gas and dust called the **coma** around the nucleus. A nucleus that is only a few miles (kilometers) wide can produce a coma that is 62,000 miles (100,000 km) across.

The closer the comet gets to the Sun, the more gases are produced. Solar winds given off by the Sun blow the gas and dust, forming a long tail that trails behind the comet. The tail of the comet can be over 62 million miles (100 million km) long. When sunlight strikes the coma and tail of the comet, the light is reflected and becomes visible to people on Earth. It's hard to believe that such a spectacular show in the sky is caused by such a small frozen mixture.

Comets are much more spectacular than the small streaks of light in the sky we call shooting stars. Shooting stars aren't stars either. They're meteors, which are particles of space dust that burn up as they enter Earth's atmosphere.

COSMIC SCIENCE IN ACTION

The most famous comet is Halley's comet, named after English astronomer Edmund Halley (1656–1742). Halley studied comets that passed by Earth in 1531, 1607, and 1682 and found that their orbits were almost identical. This discovery led him to conclude that these comets were really a single comet that orbits the Sun. He believed the comet's orbit took approximately 75 years and predicted it would return in 1758. After it appeared on schedule, it was named Halley's comet. Halley's comet has been observed 30 times since 239 B.C., most recently in 1985–86. When is the next time it will pass by?

Project 2
STAR PICTURES

Humans have always studied the stars. Thousands of years ago, when early astronomers looked at the stars at night, they drew imaginary pictures around groups of stars in the shapes of animals, people, and other objects. These star pictures are called **constellations**. Try the following activity to make your own constellation.

Materials

pencil
sheet of typing paper

Procedure

1. Draw eight dots randomly on the paper. These represent eight stars in one part of the sky.

2. Look carefully at your stars. Do they form the shape of an animal or other object?

3. Draw the object that you see. Connect the stars in a dot-to-dot manner to help you see the object.

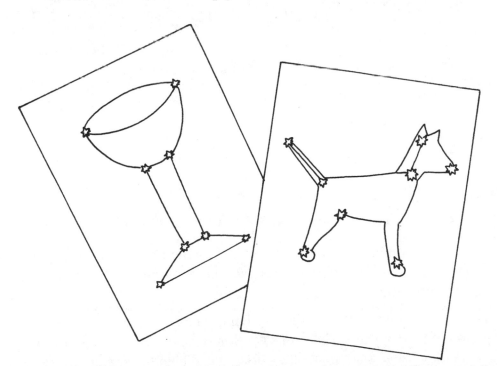

There are many myths (old, traditional stories) about the constellations. Check out a library book that tells the myths of the constellations. Write your own myth to go along with your constellation.

Explanation

Early astronomers made up the constellations thousands of years ago, just as you made up your constellation. The constellations and the myths about them made groups of stars easier to remember.

If you live in the Northern Hemisphere you will see different constellations from those you would see if you lived in the Southern Hemisphere. Because Earth revolves around the Sun, certain constellations appear only in the summer while others appear only in the winter.

Project 3
TRUE NORTH

Polaris, also called the North Star, can always be seen in the northern sky. Try the following activity to learn how to find it.

Materials

directional compass

adult helper

Procedure

NOTE: This activity should be done outdoors on a clear night.

1. Lay the compass flat on your hand, allowing the needle to spin freely. When the needle stops, it will be pointing north. Look in that direction at the sky.

2. Locate the constellation the Big Dipper in the northern part of the sky. The Big Dipper is a constellation of seven stars that looks like a ladle. Three stars make the curved handle and four stars make

the corners of the ladle's bowl. The star next to the end of the Big Dipper's handle is actually two stars.

3. Find the two stars on the outer end of the Big Dipper's bowl. Follow these two stars, call the Pointers, up directly to a star of average brightness. This is Polaris, the North Star.

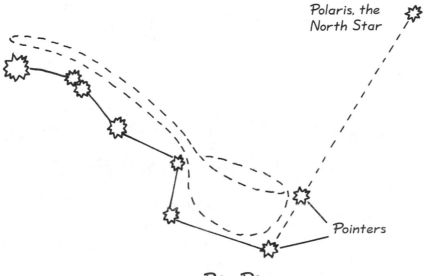

Polaris, the North Star

Pointers

Big Dipper

MORE FUN STUFF TO DO

Check out of the library an astronomy book that contains information about other constellations. Use the book to help you locate other famous constellations such as Draco, the Dragon; Taurus, the Bull; or Leo, the Lion.

Explanation

Because Earth spins on its axis, the North Pole always points in the same direction. Polaris is called the North Star because it is located almost directly above the North Pole. For years, people used the North Star and other constellations to navigate.

If you watch the stars on any night, you will see that the whole dome of the sky seems to move from east to west. The stars appear to move as a group, always keeping the same relative position in relation to one another. But the sky dome isn't actually moving. The spinning of Earth on its axis causes the sky dome to appear to turn. The stars and constellations visible in the night sky will vary from one season to the next as Earth orbits the Sun. Some stars and constellations are mainly visible in the summer, while others are mainly visible in the winter. Some, like the Big Dipper, are clearly visible all year round. Stars do move, but so slowly that it takes thousands of years for any changes to occur in the night sky.

Project 4
MARSHMALLOW CONSTELLATION

A famous constellation called Orion, the Hunter, resembles a hunter wearing a belt and sword. Orion is one of the brightest constellations in the sky. It appears in the northern sky in the winter and the southern sky in the summer. Try the following activity to learn more about the constellation Orion.

Materials

7 uncooked spaghetti noodles
ruler
7 small marshmallows
6-by-9-by-1-inch (15-by-22.5-by-2.5-cm) piece of Styrofoam

Procedure

1. Break the spaghetti pieces so that they are the following lengths: 1 inch (2.5 cm), 3 inches (7.5 cm), 3½ inches (8.75 cm), 5 inches (12.5 cm), 6 inches (15 cm), 9 inches (22.5 cm) and 10 inches (25 cm).

2. Attach a small marshmallow to one end of each piece of spaghetti. The marshmallows on the spaghetti pieces represent the following stars in the constellation Orion:

   • The marshmallow on the 1-inch (2.5-cm) spaghetti piece represents Saiph.

- The marshmallow on the 3-inch (7.5-cm) spaghetti piece represents Alnilam.

- The marshmallow on the 3½-inch (8.75-cm) spaghetti piece represents Alnitak.

- The marshmallow on the 5-inch (12.5-cm) spaghetti piece represents Mintaka.

- The marshmallow on the 6-inch (15-cm) spaghetti piece represents Rigel.

- The marshmallow on the 9-inch (22.5-cm) spaghetti piece represents Bellatrix.

- The marshmallow on the 10-inch (25-cm) spaghetti piece represents Betelgeuse.

3. Using the diagram to guide you, stick the spaghetti pieces into the Styrofoam block to make a model of Orion.

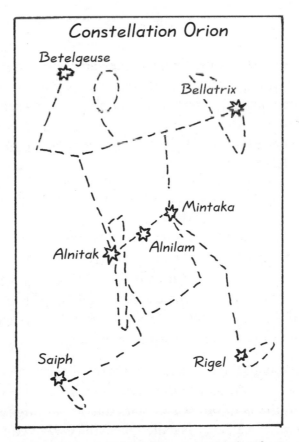

4. Look at your model of Orion. Can you think of one reason why some stars in the sky are brighter than others?

MORE FUN STUFF TO DO

On a clear winter's night, see whether you can find the stars that make up the constellation Orion. (You may need an astronomy book to help you.) Its stars Betelgeuse (pronounced "beetle juice") and Rigel both are among the brightest in the sky. Orion is located in the southern sky. The three stars of Orion's Belt can be found by following the Little Dipper's handle outward.

Don't be disappointed if you do not find all the stars that make up Orion. Some can appear to be quite dim. If the night is very clear, you may be able to see the Orion Nebula, a cloud of gas and dust out of which new stars are forming. It is located below Orion's Belt, near his "sword."

Explanation

The lengths of the spaghetti pieces represent the distances of each star from Earth. The stars on the longer pieces are closer to Earth, and those on the shorter pieces are farther away. As you can see from the model, stars in a constellation are not all on a single surface like dots on a piece of paper. Although the stars that make up a constellation like Orion appear in the same part of the sky, they are not all the same distance from Earth.

The distance to many of the stars we see is so great that it seems beyond belief. Betelgeuse is the closest star in the constellation Orion, but the light from Betelgeuse travels for 354 years before it reaches us We say that Betelgeuse is 354 light-years (ly) away from us. (A **light-year** is the distance light travels in 1 year, about 5.87 trillion miles [9.46 trillion km]). Betelgeuse is actually closer to our Sun than it is to most of the stars in Orion. Between Betelgeuse and Saiph, the farthest star in Orion, there is a distance of 1,647 ly.

Although the stars in the constellation Orion are different distances from Earth, they are all part of the same galaxy. A **galaxy** is a huge collection of millions to billions of stars that are arranged in a particular shape. Our galaxy is called the Milky Way galaxy and is shaped like a spiral. Our galaxy is just one of 100 billion galaxies in the universe.

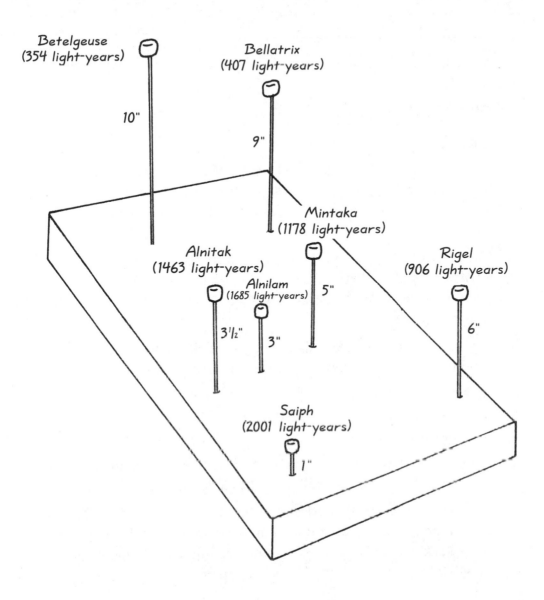

Betelgeuse
(354 light-years)

10"

Bellatrix
(407 light-years)

9"

Mintaka
(1178 light-years)

Alnitak
(1463 light-years)

Alnilam
(1685 light-years)

5"

Rigel
(906 light-years)

3½"

3"

6"

Saiph
(2001 light-years)

1"

Project 5
WOBBLE STAR

Do other stars we see at night have planets orbiting them as our sun
does? Try the following activity to learn one method scientists use to
predict which stars have planets.

Materials

scissors

tape measure

string

basketball
transparent tape
tennis ball
yardstick (meterstick)

Procedure

1. Cut a 45-inch (114-cm) piece of string. Make a loop around the basketball with the string, leaving about 6 inches (15 cm) of string at the end. Tie the string together at the top of the ball and tape it in place.

2. Cut a 24-inch (60-cm) piece of string. Make a loop around the tennis ball with the string, leaving about 12 inches (30 cm) of string at the end. Tie the string together at the top of the ball and tape it in place.

3. Tie the balls to opposite ends of the yardstick (meterstick). When you hold the stick horizontally, the centers of each ball should be directly across from each other.

4. Cut a 6-inch (15-cm) piece of string. Tie it loosely around the stick near the basketball.

5. Hold the stick by the free string only. Slide the free string nearer to or farther from the basketball until the stick balances.

6. Holding the free string, push the tennis ball so that it begins to spin around the basketball as if it were in orbit. Observe what happens to the basketball. Can you guess how this might help scientists know which stars have planets circling them?

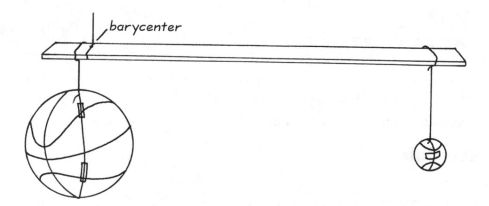

barycenter

Explanation

When Earth orbits the Sun, most people think that it makes a circle around the Sun while the Sun stands still. Actually, both objects orbit a point that is the center of their combined masses called the **barycenter**.

In this activity, the basketball has a much greater mass than the tennis ball, just as the Sun has a much greater mass than Earth. The barycenter is the point where the free string is located when the system is balanced. The barycenter is closer to the basketball, so the smaller object appears to orbit the larger object. However, the larger object does move a little, wobbling as it orbits the barycenter in small circles. When astronomers search the **universe** (our galaxy and everything else in space) for stars that have planets orbiting them, they look for this wobbling movement.

COSMIC SCIENCE IN ACTION

In 1996, two San Francisco State University astronomers, Geoffrey Marcy and Paul Butler, noticed a wobble in a star in the constellation Big Dipper. The star is 47 Ursae Majoris, 200 trillion miles (322 trillion km) from Earth. The star's wobble led them to discover a planet orbiting the star.

The planet, about twice the size of Jupiter, probably consists mostly of poisonous gases such as hydrogen sulfide, ammonia, and methane. Yet water exists even in these extreme conditions, and scientists believe that some sort of life may be present.

Project 6
TURNING RED

The wobble in a star is difficult to see because even the closest star is millions of miles (kilometers) away. How can astronomers tell whether a star wobbles? Try the next activity to see how.

Materials

street with cars

Procedure

CAUTION: Do not step out into the street.

1. Stand on the sidewalk next to the street.

2. Pick a car. Listen to the sound it makes as it drives toward you, passes you, and then drives away from you. What did you notice about the sound?

3. Close your eyes. Can you tell whether a car is moving toward you or away from you without looking?

Explanation

All sounds are actually vibrations that travel in waves, called **sound waves**. The number of times a wave occurs in a given length of time is called its **frequency**. High-frequency waves have shorter **wavelengths** (the distance between two wave crests) than low-frequency waves do. (A crest is the highest point on a wave, while a **trough** is the lowest point on a wave.)

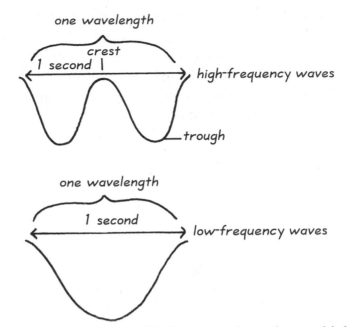

The sound waves from a car driving toward you have a higher frequency and shorter wavelength than the sound waves from a car driving away. This is called the Doppler effect. The **Doppler effect** is the difference in frequency of waves when an object approaches or moves away from an observer. When a moving object is coming toward you, the sound waves are closer together and have a higher frequency than if the object were not moving. The sound waves from an object moving away from you are farther apart and have a lower frequency than if the object were not moving. The Doppler effect lets scientists know the direction in which an object is moving without seeing it.

Like sound, light also travels in waves. The Doppler effect is true for light. The light from a star moving toward Earth has a higher frequency and shorter wavelength than a star that is not moving toward Earth. High-frequency, short-wavelength light waves look slightly blue. The light from a star moving away from Earth has a lower frequency and longer wavelength than a star that is not moving away from Earth. Low-frequency, long-wavelength light waves look slightly red. Stars that wobble look alternately slightly red, then slightly blue. Scientists measure these subtle color changes to determine the amount of the wobble. From the wobble, scientists can figure out the size of the planet that orbits the star and the radius of the planet's orbit. (The **radius** is the distance from the star to the planet.)

This subtle color change in stars can be used to answer another important question. For years, scientists and astronomers wondered whether the universe is getting bigger or smaller. Are the stars in the universe moving toward or away from us? By carefully observing many stars, scientists measured a slight red shift in their colors, similar to the slight red color wobbling stars have. The stars are moving away from us. The universe is expanding.

Glossary

accelerate   To speed up.

acceleration   An increase in speed.

acid   A sour substance with special chemical properties.

air molecules   Tiny, invisible, moving particles of air.

air pressure   The force exerted by the movement of air molecules.

air resistance   The opposing force of air molecules against a moving object.

asteroid   A small, rocky planet that orbits the Sun.

asteroid belt   A group of asteroids that travel in an orbit around the Sun between Mars and Jupiter.

astronomer   An expert in astronomy.

astronomical unit (AU)   A unit of length equal to the distance from the Sun to Earth.

astronomy   The branch of science that studies the stars, planets, and other objects in space.

atmosphere   A layer of gas that surrounds a planet.

autopilot   A device that steers a spacecraft or airplane automatically.

axis   An imaginary line that runs through the North and South poles of Earth.

barycenter   A point that is the center of the combined masses of one object and another, orbiting object, around which they both revolve.

Bode's law   A simple mathematical equation, popularized by Johann Bode, for finding the distance of each planet from the Sun.

buoyant   Capable of floating.

calcium   An important mineral in the body that makes bones strong.

carbon dioxide   The gas we naturally breathe out.

cartilage   Tough, elastic animal tissue.

centrifugal force   The force that appears to push outward on a rotating object but is really inertia trying to make a moving object continue to move in a straight-line path.

centripetal force The force that moves an object inward to keep it moving in a circle.

chemical reaction A change in matter in which substances break apart to produce one or more new substances.

coma A cloud of gas and dust that forms around the nucleus of a comet as it moves toward the Sun.

comet A giant icy lump that forms a coma around its nucleus as it moves toward the Sun.

compress To push together.

constellations Stars grouped into imaginary patterns or pictures.

contract To squeeze together.

convert To change from one form to another.

crater Bowl-shaped imprint formed by the impact of an object hitting a surface.

crescent A curved edge of the visible Moon.

crest The highest point, such as the top of a hill or wave.

diameter The distance between the endpoints of a line passing through the center of an object.

Doppler effect The difference in frequency of waves when an object approaches or moves away from an observer.

elastic energy The potential energy stored in an object when its shape is changed by either stretching or compressing.

ellipse An oval-shaped figure.

energy The ability to do work.

escape velocity The speed needed to escape a planet's gravity.

esophagus The tube that connects the mouth to the stomach.

force A push or pull on an object.

frequency The number of times a wave occurs in a given length of time.

friction A force that slows down or stops the surfaces of objects from sliding over each other.

fulcrum A fixed point on a lever.

***g* (gravity)** A unit of force equal to the force exerted by Earth's gravity on an object at rest.

galaxy   A large collection of millions to hundreds of billions of stars that has a particular shape.

gravity   The force of attraction between two objects due to their mass.

gravity assist   A technique that uses the pull of a planet's gravity on a space probe to change the probe's speed and direction; also called **gravity boost**.

gravity boost   See **gravity assist**.

gyroscope   A wheel or disk mounted to spin rapidly about an axis.

gyroscopic effect   A property of a spinning object that makes it more stable than an object that isn't spinning.

heading   The direction in which a spacecraft or airplane is going.

hypothesis   An educated guess about the results of an experiment one is going to perform.

inertia   The tendency of objects to remain either at rest or in motion unless acted on by an outside force.

kinetic energy   The energy of moving objects.

law of inertia   A law of motion that states that an object at rest stays at rest and an object in motion stays in motion unless acted on by an outside force.

lever   A simple machine made up of a rigid board or bar that is supported at a fulcrum.

light-year (ly)   The distance light travels in 1 year, about 5.87 trillion miles (9.46 trillion km).

loading bay   The part of the space shuttle where cargo is carried.

luminosity   The total power output from any sun or star.

lunar   Of or relating to the Moon.

magnetic force   The attracting or repelling force between a magnet and certain metals or other magnetic substances.

mass   The amount of matter in an object.

meteor   A space particle that burns up as it enters an atmosphere, producing a streak of light; also called a **shooting star**.

meteorite   A space particle that does not burn up in the atmosphere and strikes a planet's or moon's surface.

methane   A gas commonly called natural gas.

mineral   A nonliving, naturally occurring substance.

moon   An object that travels around a planet. The Moon is a spinning ball of rock and is a natural satellite of Earth.

National Aeronautics and Space Administration (NASA)   The organization that oversees the U.S. space program.

navigate   To steer a course for.

Newton's three laws of motion   Three laws put forward by Isaac Newton that state how objects move. (1) An object at rest will stay at rest and an object in motion will stay in motion unless acted on by an outside force. (2) An object will move with an acceleration equal to the force applied to it. (3) For every action, there is an equal and opposite reaction.

Northern Hemisphere   The top half of Earth.

North Pole   The northernmost point of Earth.

nuclear fusion   A reaction that occurs in the center of stars by which hydrogen gas changes into helium gas and releases energy in the form of heat and light.

nucleus   Center.

opportunity   The exact time a spacecraft must be launched from Earth so that the target planet will be in just the right position for the spacecraft to reach it.

orbit   The circular or elliptical path of a body around another body; to move in a circular or elliptical path around a body.

parachute   An umbrella-shaped device that slows an object's fall from a great height.

planet   An object that travels around a star.

potential energy   Stored energy.

propel   To move forward.

radius   The distance from a star to a planet in orbit around it.

reflect   To bounce back.

revolve   To move in a curved path or orbit.

rocket   An engine that burns chemicals to produce hot gases that escape through a rear opening and propel the rocket forward.

rotate   To turn or spin around a center point.

satellite   A natural or man-made object that orbits a planet.

scientific method   A method of investigating a problem in which one begins with a hypothesis, tests it with an experiment, analyzes the results, and draws a conclusion.

simple machine   A device that helps one to do work more easily.

shooting star   A small streak of light in the night sky that is actually a meteor.

solar system   A star with planets and other objects traveling around it. Our solar system is made up of the Sun with nine planets (Mercury, Venus, Earth, Mars, Jupiter, Saturn, Uranus, Neptune, and Pluto) and other smaller space objects traveling around it.

sound waves   Vibrations that travel in waves to produce sounds that we can hear.

South Pole   The southernmost point of Earth.

space capsule   The top part of a rocket that holds the astronauts.

space probe   An unmanned spacecraft that collects information.

space station   A large satellite orbiting Earth with room on board for people to work and live.

star   A spinning ball of hot gas that releases energy in the form of heat and light.

stretch   To pull apart.

sun   A star in the center of a solar system. Our sun is called the Sun.

telescope   A tubelike instrument that uses lenses to make distant objects appear nearer and larger.

transfer orbit   An orbit around the Sun that is the most energy-efficient way to travel between planets in our solar system.

trough   The lowest point on a wave.

universe   Our galaxy and everything else in space.

vertebrae   The 26 linked bones that make up the human spine.

watt   The unit used to measure power.

wavelength   The distance between two wave crests.

weight   The force with which objects are pulled toward Earth by gravity.

Index